CHINA ROOT

Other Books by David Hinton

WRITING

Awakened Cosmos (Essay)
Desert (Poetry)
The Wilds of Poetry (Essay)
Existence: A Story (Essay)
Hunger Mountain (Essay)
Fossil Sky (Poetry)

TRANSLATION

The Selected Poems of Tu Fu
No-Gate Gateway
I Ching
The Late Poems of Wang An-shih
The Four Chinese Classics
Classical Chinese Poetry
The Selected Poems of Wang Wei
The Mountain Poems of Meng Hao-jan
Mountain Home
The Mountain Poems of Hsieh Ling-yün
Tao Te Ching
The Selected Poems of Po Chü-i
The Analects
Mencius
Chuang Tzu: The Inner Chapters
The Late Poems of Meng Chiao
The Selected Poems of Li Po
The Selected Poems of T'ao Ch'ien

PRAISE FOR
China Root

"China Root is an utterly engrossing account of the deepest treasures the Zen/Ch'an path can open up, as it leads us into the manifest-yet-hidden wonders of who we really are. Hinton writes as very few can, not only as a scholar, practitioner, and translator but also as a poet—something the old artist-intellectuals of China would surely have appreciated. His deep understanding of the Taoist roots of Ch'an shine a light on the Zen practice of today, taking us back in a thrilling way beyond the Japanese rigor and aesthetics, beyond the mythical T'ang Dynasty flourishing of Ch'an's great ancestors, back to its Taoist roots in the first millennium B.C.E.—and even beyond them, into the mists of its paleolithic origins. It is here, back in its true roots—which also happen to be the deepest aspects of our life—that Hinton beautifully makes clear our participation in a generative cosmos, a constantly manifesting, burgeoning Presence, even while it never ceases to be a primordial Absence.

Oddly perhaps, in spite of Hinton's expert parsing out of missteps in the translation and transmission of this Dharma to the West, I can't help feeling I've just read a staggeringly good account of the modern Zen training a contemporary Japanese-based lineage led me through. Be that as it may, this thoroughly gripping book pulls together various threads of David Hinton's prior work into one powerful, concise masterwork. May it echo through modern zendos for decades to come."

—HENRY SHUKMAN ROSHI, author of
One Blade of Grass: A Zen Memoir

CHINA ROOT

Taoism, Ch'an, and
Original Zen

David Hinton

SHAMBHALA

Shambhala Publications, Inc.
2129 13th Street
Boulder, Colorado 80302
www.shambhala.com

© 2020 by David Hinton

Cover art: *Narcissus*, Zhao Mengjian, mid-13th century,
Ex coll.: C. C. Wang Family, Gift of The Dillon Fund, 1973
Cover design: Erin Seaward-Hiatt
Interior design: Steve Dyer

Image on p. 24 courtesy of Freer Gallery of Art, Smithsonian Institution,
Washington, D.C.: Purchase—funds provided by the B. Rhodes and
Leona B. Carpenter Foundation in honor of the 75th Anniversary
of the Freer Gallery of Art, F1998.27

9 8 7 6 5 4

Printed in the United States of America

Shambhala Publications makes every effort to print on acid-free,
recycled paper.
Shambhala Publications is distributed worldwide
by Penguin Random House, Inc., and its subsidiaries.

LIBRARY OF CONGRESS CATALOGING-IN-PUBLICATION DATA
Names: Hinton, David, 1954– author.
Title: China root: Taoism, Ch'an, and original Zen / David Hinton.
Description: First edition. | Boulder, Colorado: Shambhala, 2020. |
Includes bibliographical references.
Identifiers: LCCN 2019056448 | ISBN 9781611807134 (trade paperback)
Subjects: LCSH: Zen Buddhism—China—Essence, genius, nature. | Zen
Buddhism—Relations—Taoism. | Taoism—Relations—Zen Buddhism .
Classification: LCC BQ9262.9.C5 H72 2020 | DDC 294.3/9270951—dc23
LC record available at https://lccn.loc.gov/2019056448

CONTENTS

III

CHINA ROOT

INTRODUCTION

WHAT HAPPENS IF WE DISMANTLE ALL OF OUR human conceptual constructions, all of the explanations and assumptions that structure consciousness and orient us and define us as centers of identity? To do that not in the abstract, but at the level of immediate experience. What would that leave us? What might we discover about ourselves at levels deeper than the contingent histories and thoughts that define us as identity-centers? And what would it mean about the texture of everyday experience?

This dismantling is the adventure of Ch'an (Jap. Zen) Buddhism as originally practiced in ancient China, and its primary revelation is the larger self or "original-nature" that remains after the deconstruction. The awakening that Ch'an cultivated was 見性: "seeing original-nature" (chien-hsing; Jap. kensho). And in cultivating this awakening, Ch'an's sage-masters operated like a wrecking-crew disassembling every possible story or explanation, idea or assumption or certainty. The Ch'an conceptual world sounds like a constellation of answers, a clear account of consciousness and Cosmos and their interrelation, and it is. But in the end, Ch'an dismantles all of our answers, including its own, to leave a new way of being.

1

The T'ang Dynasty Ch'an master Yellow-Bitterroot Mountain (Huang Po: died 850) compared this dismantling to "clearing away shit-piles." It is the cultivation of a remarkably rich and even ecstatic kind of freedom—though the nature of that liberation depends upon the stories and ideas that are deconstructed, hence the need to understand them first. Ch'an is not simply about establishing a mind of tranquility: that happens, but in unexpected ways. Instead, by emptying consciousness of the isolated identity-center we take for granted in our daily lives, Ch'an intends to liberate us into a larger identity that is woven integrally into landscape, earth, and Cosmos. This is Ch'an awakening: a radical kind of liberation, a freedom that transforms everything from identity and immediate everyday experience to death itself. And it demands a wild and fearless mind.

The Ch'an adventure answers a sense of rootless exile caused by a fundamental rupture between oneself and everything else—a sense of alienation that structures consciousness much more radically in our modern world than in ancient China. The great sangha-case (koan) collection *No-Gate Gateway* (1228 C.E.) poetically describes this as living "a ghost's life, clinging to weeds and trees." It is a sense of not being present in one's immediate life-experience or of being caught in some inside radically separated from the vast outside of empirical reality, together with a suspicion that it needn't be this way, that some kind of immediacy and wholeness is possible.

That wholeness was the original human condition, a fact central to Ch'an thought and practice. Ch'an is, as we will see, a return of consciousness to this primal cultural level: hence, Ch'an's cultivation of awakening as a reinhabiting of the "original-nature" of consciousness. Humankind's primal wholeness began to fade during the Paleolithic, when people slowly became self-reflective and aware of themselves as separate from the rest of existence. It was a period when humans were still rooted in natural process and yet separate enough to produce a rich artistic and spiritual tradition. But that incipient separation eventually became a rupture in agrarian Neolithic culture, when people began settling into villages (permanent enclaves separate from the landscape) and began controlling "nature" in the form of domesticated plants and animals: a detached instrumentalist relationship to the world.

The advent of alphabetic writing completed this transformation. In primal cultures, language (existing only as thought or speech) and all mental process moved the way everything else moved: appearing, evolving, disappearing. There was no fundamental separation between subjective and objective realms. But with writing, people could inscribe thoughts, making them seem permanent: they could come back to those thoughts later, and others could read those thoughts in distant times and places. Writing seems to defy the fleeting nature of our inner reality, creating the illusion of an immaterial and timeless subjective world, a mental realm of permanence that is separate from the world in a radically ontological way. Writing made mental processes seem changeless for the first time. And compounding this, words in alphabetic languages have an arbitrary relationship to the world of things, reinforcing this separation of subjectivity and the world. All of this soon led to a mythologization of that inner world as a "soul" or "spirit," part of dualistic cosmologies and theologies that divide the world into a spirit realm (soul/heaven) and a material realm (body/earth). That established the things of this world as *objects* of transcendental thought, as ontologically out there and other than us. It replaces the immediate experience of things in and of themselves with knowledge and explanation of them.

3

This process of rupture entailed a shift from the Paleolithic's gynocentric worldview to an androcentric worldview. In China, the process was complete by the historical beginnings of Chinese civilization in the Shang Dynasty (1766–1040 B.C.E.), which was indeed fiercely patriarchal. In the Shang, it was believed that all things were created and controlled by a male and all-powerful monotheistic deity very like the sky-god of Judeo-Christian theology, a deity known simply as Lord-Celestial. Everyone's ancestors lived on in a spirit realm, and they had power to influence earthly events, so people prayed and offered sacrifices to them. Lord-Celestial was the all-powerful chief of these ancestors, and he was the high ancestor of the Shang's male rulers. Hence, Lord-Celestial provided those rulers with a transcendental source of legitimacy through lineage. And it gave them god-like power, because through prayer and ritual they could influence Lord-Celestial's shaping of events. All aspects of people's lives were thus controlled by the emperor: weather, harvest, politics, economics, religion, etc. Indeed, as in the traditional West, people didn't experience themselves as substantially different from spirits, for the human realm was simply an earthly extension of the spirit realm.

Eventually, the Shang emperors grew tyrannical, and the dynasty was overthrown by the Chou Dynasty (1040–223 B.C.E.), whereupon the Chou rulers reinvented Lord-Celestial as an impersonal "Heaven," thus ending the Shang's claim to legitimacy by lineage. The Chou rulers justified their rule by claiming they had the "Mandate of Heaven," so when their rule was in turn overthrown, the last semblance of theocratic cosmology crumbled, leaving no organizing system to structure society. Philosophers like Lao Tzu and Confucius (c. fifth–sixth centuries B.C.E.) struggled to invent a new philosophical framework that could replace the spiritualistic system with a humanistic one based on empirical reality. One aspect of this transformation was the reinvention of Heaven as an entirely empirical phenomena—the generative cosmological force that drives the ongoing transformation of natural process—thereby secularizing the sacred while at the same time investing the secular with sacred dimensions: what we today would call a form of pantheism.

This transition moment was soon superseded by an entirely secular concept: Tao (道), which was essentially synonymous with "heaven," but without the metaphysical implications. Tao is the central concept in Taoism as formulated in the I Ching (c. second millennium B.C.E.) and Lao Tzu's Tao Te Ching (c. sixth century B.C.E.)—poetic texts that are the seminal works in Chinese spiritual philosophy, and the deepest root-source of Ch'an thought and practice. Indeed, Taoist ontology/cosmology supplies the conceptual framework that shapes Ch'an at its foundational levels. As we will see in the first chapter, Lao Tzu uses the term Tao to describe the empirical Cosmos as a single living tissue that is inexplicably generative in its very nature. Belonging to this magical tissue made the world of immediate experience wholly mysterious and wondrous and sufficient in and of itself. There was no longer a need to invest reality with imagined dimensions of the sacred or divine.

Lao Tzu's vision apparently derives from a primal tradition that persisted outside the theocratic power structures of the Shang and Chou dynasties. Even here at the beginning of Chinese philosophy, there was a longing for a primal past. And indeed, like the I Ching, the Tao Te Ching seems to have been largely constructed from fragments handed down in an oral wisdom-tradition. As such, it represents a return to the earliest levels of proto-Chinese culture: to the Paleolithic, it seems,

5

where the empirical Cosmos was recognized as female in its fundamental nature, as a magisterial and perpetually generative organism in constant transformation. In fact, Lao Tzu often refers to Tao as *female* or *mother*. This is the root of a remarkable fact: high Chinese civilization, for all its complexity and sophistication, never forgot its origins in a gynocentric primitive. Indeed, the primitive was the very thing responsible for the distinctive nature of its complexity and sophistication. Ch'an is integral to that cultural complex, and only when it's seen this way can it (or contemporary Zen) really be understood.

American Zen generally sees its tradition as a stream of Buddhism that began in India, passed through China (with some significant developments), then through Japan (where it became known as Zen, the Japanese pronunciation for the *Ch'an* ideogram, and developed further), and then twelve centuries later passed on to America, where the tradition is primarily shaped by its Japanese antecedent. This narrative involves a stunning project of cultural appropriation in which Ch'an is presented as if it were Japanese: the names of Chinese Ch'an masters have been widely rendered in Japanese, as have important terminology including *zen, koan, kensho, satori, mu*.

That story isn't wrong, but it leaves out just about everything that matters to Ch'an. It would be more accurate to say that when Buddhism arrived in China during the first century of the current era, it was fundamentally reinterpreted and reshaped by Taoist thought, its more abstract metaphysical sensibility becoming grounded in an earthly and empirically based vision. The result of this amalgam, which began to take shape from the third into the fifth centuries c.e., is Ch'an. And in this transformation, Buddhism is so transformed by

6

Taoist thought that, aside from a few institutional trappings, it is scarcely recognizable as Buddhism at all.

But it may be still more accurate to simply say that the influence of Buddhism pushed native Chinese philosophy to a new level of clarity and intensity, for the originators of Ch'an essentially adopted aspects of Buddhism (texts, ideas, practices) that they found useful in enriching their own Taoist understanding, while reconceiving them fundamentally in Taoist terms. Most important among these imported Buddhist elements was a central focus on the nature of empty-mind, consciousness emptied of all content, a focus cultivated through a highly developed practice of empty-mind meditation known as *dhyana*. As we will see, Ch'an found *dhyana* meditation a useful stage in training, but at more advanced levels reconceived and in the end dismantled it, returning to an enriched version of ancient Taoism's concept of meditation. And Buddhism functions more generally as a conceptual framework to dismantle—part of the Ch'an adventure of razing all conceptual constructions. This imperative to disassemble ideas was certainly present in the forms of Buddhism that arrived in China, part of why it appealed to China's artist-intellectuals. But Ch'an deconstruction operates very differently because it was primarily inherited from early Taoism. In the end, Buddhism is only a scrim on the surface of Ch'an. At depth, Ch'an's deconstructive project extends a tradition of demolition that was the essence of Taoism from its origins in the *Tao Te Ching*, and the end result of the dismantling is defined by the earthy Taoist/Ch'an conceptual framework.

So Ch'an was less Buddhism than a rebellion against Buddhism. And in the end, it is most accurately described not as Buddhism reconfigured by Taoism, but as Taoism reconfigured by a Buddhism that was dismantled and discarded after

7

the reconfiguration was complete. This is how ancient China's artist-intellectual class saw it: Ch'an as a refinement and extension of Taoism. Indeed, the more Ch'an is seen at the deep levels essential for awakening, the more Taoist is looks; while the more it is seen at shallow or institutional levels, the more Buddhist it looks.

The relationship also evolved historically. The earlier we look in Ch'an's development, the more we find references to imported Buddhism, its texts, terminologies, rituals, practices: because Chinese intellectuals were struggling to understand what this new system of thought offered to their own Taoist framework, and also because the more conventional- and institutional-minded among them wanted to empower themselves with a venerable and exotic authority. On the other hand, the later in Ch'an history we look, the more assured thinkers and practitioners were in their practice and understanding, the less frequent such references are, and the more problematized they are. In mature Ch'an, such references were generally mere storytelling or poetic play—often used to engage conventionally minded students who were steeped in Buddhist terminologies and concepts. But it was more fundamentally part of a strategy to set up Buddhism as a framework of understanding and certainty to be ridiculed and dismantled. For the deconstruction of such conceptual structures is Ch'an's most essential characteristic, its radical path of liberation.

In part, this reconfiguration and incorporation of *dhyana* Buddhism into Taoism was the result of translation. The first and most important aspect of this is what we might now call poor translation. Sanskrit terms were generally (mis-)translated into native Taoist terms, hence transforming Indian Buddhist concepts into Taoist concepts. The second way translation domesticated imported Indian concepts derives from the unique

8

fact that Chinese is not alphabetic, so it cannot simply incorporate Sanskrit terms into Chinese. Instead, it must transliterate them with Chinese ideograms having similar sounds. In Chinese, each available sound is used to pronounce many different ideograms (unlike English where each word is generally pronounced differently from all other words)—so there were choices for each Sanskrit sound needing transliteration. In making those choices within their own Taoist philosophical framework, scholars often chose meanings that added new, more native Chinese dimensions to the Indian concepts. *Samadhi*, meaning in Indian Buddhism "consciousness emptied of all subjective content," becomes in Chinese the suggestively elemental "three-shadowed earth" (三昧地). *Tathagata*, a name for Buddha as the "thus-come or thus-perfected one," becomes "existence-tissue arrival" (如來). And *dhyana* ("meditation") becomes *Ch'an* (禪) itself, which originally meant "altar" and "sacrifice to rivers-and-mountains," and we will see that its etymology suggests "the Cosmos alone simply and exhaustively with itself."

Ch'an's native sources can also be seen in the literary forms taken by Ch'an texts, which grew out of forms developed much earlier in the Chinese tradition. In their fragmentary and paradoxical nature, Ch'an texts continue the forms developed by early Taoist sages in the *Tao Te Ching* and *Chuang Tzu* (sixth and fourth centuries B.C.E.). Texts recording the teachings of Ch'an masters, often as interactions with students, continue a form developed in the Confucian *Analects* (sixth century B.C.E.) Philosophy through storytelling (rather than abstract system-building) is typical of all those ancient Chinese books, as it is in the literature of Ch'an. And finally, Ch'an's poetry and poetic compression in prose grew out of a culture for which poetry was central and universally practiced by artist-intellectuals.

9

As a refinement of Taoism, Ch'an came to define the conceptual framework of China's artist-intellectuals. It became that framework's most clear and distilled and highly developed expression. Ch'an masters were generally a part of that artist-intellectual class. They received the same classical education, and they associated broadly with artist-intellectuals who themselves generally practiced Ch'an in some form. The Ch'an monastery was a permeable intellectual center, allowing fluid movement in and out. Monks often visited artist-intellectuals, and those artist-intellectuals often visited monasteries to see friends, practice, and consult Ch'an masters. In addition, when traveling far from home, they often stopped at monasteries, which functioned as inns.

Like all aspects of high Chinese culture (philosophy, the arts, government), Ch'an was exclusive to the artist-intellectual class, and it had little in common with the myriad forms of religious Buddhism practiced by the illiterate masses. And at its core levels, it was little concerned with the Bodhisattva ideal of compassion and social responsibility, as that was the realm of Confucianism. (The mind of artist-intellectuals had two aspects in ancient China: the socially engaged Confucian, which they pursued in their work as government bureaucrats; and the spiritual Taoist, which they pursued in their private lives.) These artist-intellectuals saw Ch'an not as religion or an institution dedicated to social work, but as a philosophical practice that cultivates profound insight into the empirical nature of consciousness and Cosmos. And their creative work was deeply influenced by Ch'an. In fact, poetry, calligraphy, and painting were broadly considered forms of Ch'an practice and teaching.

The historical process of cultural transformation that created Taoism and Ch'an is very similar to what has happened in the West over the last few centuries: the collapse of a monotheistic framework, passing through a phase of pantheism (Deism and Romanticism), and ending in our current secular scientific worldview. China was almost three thousand years ahead of the West in this regard, and their innovations are informative because they are radically free of the fundamental assumptions that still shape Western thought. The Chinese model is particularly relevant to our contemporary situation for a number of reasons. First, it is empirically based, insights coming not from belief or abstract speculation, but from close attention to the deep nature of cosmological process and our everyday experience. And so, it comports with modern scientific understanding, while adding an empirical phenomenology far more powerful and nuanced than anything found in Western culture. Second, it is profoundly gynocentric, a cosmology that sees the Cosmos as female in its essence and whose deep sources lie in oral wisdom-traditions of gynocentric Paleolithic cultures. Third, it is what we might now call "deep-ecology," meaning it weaves human consciousness into the "natural world" at the most fundamental levels, a radical alternative to our culture's traditional assumptions.

These elements define the awakening offered by Ch'an Buddhism. That awakening is a radical freedom that opens when conceptual structures are deconstructed, when we "cut off the mind-road," as *No-Gate Gateway*'s poetic image-making puts it: "if you don't cut off the mind-road, you live a ghost's life, clinging to weeds and trees." Hence the famous Ch'an principle that understanding resides outside words and ideas. But the nature of that freedom is in fact defined by the very words and ideas Ch'an dismantles: the native philosophical assumptions that shaped consciousness for ancient China's artist-intellectuals, and that are largely absent for Western practitioners. But it appears that in its migration to Japan and, over a millennium later, from Japan to America, Ch'an's native philosophical framework was largely forgotten, for it is all but absent in modern American teaching texts and translations of the original Ch'an literature. (This problem and how it is addressed in this book are explained in the Reader's Note that follows this Introduction.)

We know the original Ch'an teachings through texts. Even when translated accurately, the teachings in those texts can seem hermetic and perplexing—but once we understand the Taoist/Ch'an framework, they become much more forthcoming and approachable. Ch'an's essentials are summarized in a remarkably concise poem attributed to Bodhidharma (died c. 530),* who is by legend the First Patriarch of Ch'an and a seminal figure in the origin of Ch'an as a body of thought and practice:

---

* As with most originary figures of Chinese philosophy—Lao Tzu, Chuang Tzu, Confucius—a number of seminal Ch'an figures appear to have evolved over time. Texts recording their lives and teachings only took shape after their deaths, and those texts tended to grow and change over time as new accounts were edited and rewritten. It's impossible to know how accurate or inaccurate such records are: huge numbers of ancient Chinese texts were lost, not to mention notes taken by students, so direct connections to contemporaneous accounts cannot be ruled out. Also, Ch'an was largely an oral tradition, so a great deal of a teacher's record could have been handed down orally with reasonable accuracy. In any case, those constructed figures and their teachings are in fact what defines the Ch'an tradition. So, this book will speak of them and the records of their teachings the way they came to be understood by the Ch'an community in ancient China: as representing actual historical figures and their teachings.

12

A separate transmission outside all teaching
and not founded in fine words of scripture,

it's simple: pointing directly at mind. There,
seeing original-nature, you become Buddha.

教	外	別	傳
teaching	outside	separate	transmission
不	立	文	字
not	founded	elegant	words
直	指	人	心
direct	pointing	person	mind
見	性	成	佛
see	original-nature	become	Buddha

But to understand this, we must understand why Bodhidharma is saying these things, and just what he means by "transmission," "mind," "original-nature," and even "Buddha." Such understanding requires that we read the poem within Ch'an's native philosophical framework. Most fundamentally, that framework is Taoist ontology/cosmology, the native intellectual inheritance taken for granted by Ch'an's original practitioners. As such, it suffuses original Ch'an teaching. And tellingly, it is rarely discussed directly in Ch'an texts because the ideas were quite simply the shared assumption. But so much of Ch'an teaching *enacts* the insight of that assumed framework, for Ch'an practice was about understanding that framework not as abstract ideas, but as actual immediate experience. That meant "seeing original-nature" (見性), the term that appears as the definition of awakening not just in the last line of the Bodhidharma poem, but throughout the tradition.

China Root describes this native framework of ideas, each chapter addressing in the simplest possible way one key dimension of Ch'an thought and practice. The book also tries to show how those ideas were systematically dismantled by Taoist/Ch'an masters, and how it is this very dismantling that leads to the liberation of awakening. Understanding Zen in its ancient Ch'an form can only transform Zen practice. Once reinvested with its Taoist/Ch'an roots, it becomes not just straightforward and accessible, but also dynamic with the fertile energy of earth and Cosmos. And those roots transform generic "Zen perplexity" into an earthy mystery that can easily be inhabited in daily life. For while the central thrust of Zen practice is to be immediately present in one's life, rather than living lost in the isolate realm of thought, Zen's native Taoist/Ch'an framework adds profound and unexpected dimensions to that presence, opening the possibility of weaving consciousness into landscape, earth, Cosmos.

Ancient Chinese poems speak of mountains having roots: here is the bedrock of Zen, its *China Root*.

READER'S NOTE

THE PRIMARY PROJECT OF THIS BOOK IS A DIRECT AND philosophical one: to describe the native conceptual framework of Ch'an in ancient China, to make it available to contemporary philosophical understanding and spiritual practice. This native understanding and practice of Ch'an is largely missing in contemporary American Zen because that conceptual framework was mostly lost in Ch'an's migration from China through Japan to America. Indeed, that conceptual framework appears already lost in Japan, for little trace of it appears in the writings of the great Japanese scholar D. T. Suzuki, whose many books introduced Zen to the Western world. The reasons for this are surely complex and beyond the scope of this book. But as a generalized beginning toward that understanding, it could be said that Japan's cultural proclivity was toward paring things down to elegant essentials, a minimalist aesthetic defined by simplicity and order, stillness and emptiness. Japan sent an army of cultural figures to China beginning in the eighth century (just after the Sixth Patriarch) to master and bring to Japan all of Chinese culture: arts, philosophy, even the language itself. Over the centuries that followed, this adopted culture seems to have been pared down to

15

its minimalist essentials in every field. China's poetry based on landscape images is purified in haiku to the briefest imagistic gesture. Much the same thing happened in painting, calligraphy, architecture, and even the tea ceremony, where a formalized ritual of tranquil emptiness replaced China's relaxed Taoist practice. And it appears much the same thing happened to Ch'an, its philosophically complex and messy earthiness giving way to a clean framework of stillness and order—the institutional Zen that migrated to America and Europe.

An unavoidable secondary task for this book is to document how the various aspects of Ch'an's native understanding are misrepresented or altogether absent in the literature of American Zen. It is true that Ch'an/Zen is described as direct teaching from master to student outside of words and ideas. But again, the nature of such teachings and their goal of enlightenment is in fact defined by words and ideas, the conceptual framework within which they operate—and that framework has little to do with original Ch'an. It would be impossible to examine the private teachings of all modern American Zen teachers, but the absence of original Ch'an in the entire literature of American Zen, including all books by Zen teachers, seems good evidence that it is absent from those direct teachings as well.

To avoid disrupting *China Root*'s primary philosophical project, this secondary task is addressed in the Appendix. The near absence of original Ch'an in books about Zen (many by Zen masters) is a simple fact, and could only be documented by citing the entire literature. But Ch'an's absence in contemporary Zen can be tellingly documented in the modern translations of original Ch'an texts (many also done by Zen teachers). The Appendix compares many of the translations in this book (all of them my own) with the standard translations that have

16

shaped contemporary Zen, to show in detail how Ch'an's conceptual framework is fundamentally misrepresented or simply lost in the translations. Translations that have comparisons in the Appendix are indicated with reference numbers.

On a larger scale, I have already translated the most widely used sangha-case (koan) collection, *No-Gate Gateway* (*Wu Men Kuan*), because it displays the whole Taoist/Ch'an conceptual framework especially well, using the root terms and concepts extensively. The intent was to show Ch'an returned to its native philosophical ground, a project that I explicitly address in the book's introduction and apparatus. The distortions of previous translations can be seen by comparing passages of philosophical interest. And future translations will continue this reclamation of original Ch'an, including first a companion to this volume: a "Sourcebook of Original Zen." This sourcebook will contain selections from Ch'an's essential texts, thereby presenting Ch'an's native conceptual framework in its own words. It will also trace *China Root*'s historical argument through texts that show how Ch'an's native conceptual framework begins not in Indian Buddhism but in the early Taoist texts, and how that framework evolved through proto-Ch'an texts and on into mature Ch'an.

Finally, a note on names. Artist-intellectuals in ancient China adopted names having meanings that somehow represented their natures. This was strikingly true in the world of Ch'an, where the names adopted are especially colorful and philosophically revealing. Names are therefore translated here, rather than the usual strategy of leaving them in their untranslated romanized form (another way modern Zen translations fail to render the native world of Ch'an).

I

Tao

VIRTUALLY ALL ASPECTS OF CH'AN'S CONCEP-
tual framework are anticipated in Taoism's
seminal texts: *I Ching, Tao Te Ching, Chuang Tzu*. Much like
the distinction between Ch'an and religious Buddhism, there
were two forms of Taoism: religious Taoism that was practiced
primarily by the illiterate masses; and philosophical Taoism, the
form that artist intellectuals took seriously and that evolved
into Ch'an. This philosophical Taoism is best described as a
spiritual ecology, the central concept of which is Tao, or "Way."
Tao originally meant "way," as in "pathway" or "roadway"—a
meaning it has kept. But Lao Tzu and Chuang Tzu, the seminal
Taoist thinkers, redefined it as a generative cosmological process, an ontological path*Way* by which things come into existence, evolve through their lives, and then go out of existence,
only to be transformed and reemerge in a new form.

Tao represents one of the most dramatic indications that
conceptually Ch'an is an extension of Taoism, because the
term *Tao* is used extensively at foundational levels in Ch'an
with exactly the same meaning. In fact, Ch'an practitioners
were often called 道流: "those who follow Tao," or more

literally, "those who flow along with Tao." Bodhidharma states it quite simply: "Tao is Ch'an" (see p. 91 for the entire passage). But Tao is generally read in contemporary Zen to mean the Buddhist "way" of understanding and practice that leads to awakening—which is sometimes correct, but only sometimes. And when it is read as the philosophical concept, it is understood as some kind of vague mystical reality, perhaps only available to the awakened. But in fact, Tao in its philosophical sense is a clearly defined and straightforward idea that isn't difficult to understand. And indeed, the failure to understand Tao is perhaps the first and most fundamental way in which the original understanding of Ch'an is lost in contemporary Zen.

To understand Tao, we must approach it at its deepest ontological and cosmological level, where the distinction between Absence (無) and Presence (有) arises, foundational concepts that also frequent Ch'an texts (and are entirely lost in modern translations). Presence is simply the empirical universe, which the ancients described as the ten thousand things in constant transformation; and Absence is the generative void from which this ever-changing realm of Presence perpetually emerges. Lao Tzu describes it succinctly like this:

All beneath heaven, the ten thousand things:
it's all born of Presence,
and Presence is born of Absence.[1]

In anticipation of fuller discussions to come, it's important to understand here that Absence is not some kind of metaphysical dimension: it is instead simply the empirical Cosmos seen as a single generative tissue, while Presence is the Cosmos seen as that tissue individuated into the ten thousand distinct things constantly giving birth to new things.

In its primal generative nature, this cosmology assumes a more elemental experience of time. Not linear, the familiar metaphysical river flowing past, nor even cyclical, as time in primal cultures is imprecisely described—it is instead an all-encompassing generative present that might be described as an origin-moment/place, a constant burgeoning forth in which the ten thousand things emerge from the generative source-tissue of existence: Absence burgeoning forth into Presence. And as we will see in many different ways, inhabiting this origin-moment/place is the abiding essence of Ch'an practice.

Tao as an ongoing *Way* is simply an ontological description of natural process, perhaps manifest most immediately in the seasonal cycle: the pregnant emptiness of Absence in winter, Presence's burgeoning forth in spring, the fullness of its flourishing in summer, and its dying back into Absence in autumn. And it is visible as the deep subject matter of Chinese landscape paintings, an art form that arose with Ch'an historically and was generally considered a method of Ch'an practice and teaching. This emptiness is especially evident in the painting on the following page by Eight-Mountain Vast (Pa Ta Shan Jen), one of the most idiosyncratic of China's great painters and also a Ch'an teacher. The empty space in such paintings—mist and cloud, sky, lakewater, even elements of the landscape itself—depicts Absence, the generative emptiness from which the landscape elements (Presence) are seemingly just emerging, or into which they are just vanishing. (For an extensive account of how landscape paintings manifest Taoist/Ch'an understanding, see my book *Existence: A Story*.)

At such ontological and cosmological depths, Taoist and Ch'an thinkers struggle to find accurate descriptions and explanations. As we will see over and over, concepts inevitably overlap and blur together, emphasizing different aspects of

Pa Ta Shan Jen (1626–1705): *Landscape after Tung Yüan* (1693).
Freer-Sackler Gallery, Washington

the same fundamental concept. Absence is hard to distinguish from Tao, it just shifts the emphasis a bit. And there is another fundamental concept that also describes Tao or Absence: *ch'i* (氣). 氣 is often described as the universal life-force breathing through things. But this presumes a dualism that separates reality into matter and a breath-force (spirit) that infuses it with life. That dualism may be useful as an approach to understanding; but more fully understood, *ch'i* is both breath-force and matter simultaneously. Hence, it is nothing other than Tao or Absence, emphasizing its nature as a single tissue dynamic and generative through and through, the matter and energy of the Cosmos seen together as a single breath-force surging through its perpetual transformations.

This sense of reality as a dynamic breath-force tissue is reflected in the Chinese language itself, and so operates as an unnoticed assumption in ancient Chinese consciousness. There is no distinction between noun and verb in classical Chinese. Virtually all words can function as either. Hence, the sense of reality as verbal. a tissue alive and in process. This includes all individual elements of reality, such as mountains or people, and contrasts with our language's sense that reality is nominal, an assemblage of static things. A noun in fact only refers to a temporal slice through the ongoing verbal process that any thing actually is.

In addition, all ideograms are based on "radicals": base-elements from which a range of related words are constructed. For instance, there are hundreds of words constructed by adding various elements to the radical "water," which like most radicals is pictographic in its original form: 川, showing the rippling current of a stream or river. This system embodies the sense of interconnectedness we find in Taoism's description of reality, and the sense shared throughout Taoist/Ch'an thought that fundamental principles permeate the tissue of existence.

Sage wisdom in ancient China meant understanding the deep nature of consciousness and Cosmos, how they are woven together into a single fabric, for such understanding enables us to dwell as integral to Tao's generative cosmological process. This is the awakening of Ch'an: "seeing original-nature." As we will see, the essence of Ch'an practice is moving always at the generative origin-moment/place, for it is there that we move as integral to existence as a whole. The seminal Sixth Patriarch Prajna-Able (Hui Neng: 638–713) gave this a radical form when he said: "You can see the ten thousand dharmas within your own original-nature, for every dharma is there of itself in original-nature." He was using *dharma* to mean the things and processes that make up our Cosmos, and so was expressing an idea prefigured as far back in Chinese philosophy as Mencius (fourth century B.C.E.), who said: "The ten thousand things are all there in me. And there's no joy greater than looking within and finding myself faithful to them."

Ch'an recognized it is the presumption of a self that precludes our dwelling as integral to Tao's generative cosmological process, for self as identity-center is the structure that isolates us as fundamentally separate from the world around us. In that dwelling, we identify not with an isolate identity-center self, but with Tao in all its boundless dimensions. This is an understanding that begins with Lao Tzu, for whom liberation from the isolate self reveals the true nature of self as integral to the cosmological process of Tao: "If you aren't free of yourself / how will you ever become yourself." And in that liberation, altogether different from Buddha's transcendental extinction of self in nirvana, we find a radical freedom that is the focus of both Taoist and Ch'an practice.

26

Meditation

CH'AN PRACTICE WAS NOT SIMPLY ABOUT cultivating an abstract understanding of Taoist ontology/cosmology and the nature of consciousness; it was about actually living that understanding as a matter of immediate experience. And at the center of Ch'an practice was meditation. Indeed, Ch'an (禪), a transliteration of the Sanskrit dhyana, simply means "meditation." (The original pronunciation of 禪 was dian, which makes more sense as a transliteration; but as with most Chinese words, the pronunciation changed over time.) The term was adopted as a name because Ch'an focuses so resolutely on meditation practice as the primary path to awakening.

The philosophical Taoism of Lao Tzu and Chuang Tzu was reenergized eight centuries after its origins by a philosophical movement known as Dark-Enigma Learning, which arose in the third century C.E. when Buddhism was becoming a major influence in Chinese culture. Its two major figures, Wang Pi (226–249) and Kuo Hsiang (252–312), articulated their thought in the form of commentaries on the seminal Taoist classics: I Ching, Tao Te Ching, Chuang Tzu. In these commentaries,

27

they emphasized and deepened the ontological and cosmological dimensions of those seminal texts, and it was those dimensions that blended with newly imported Buddhism to create Ch'an. Or perhaps more accurately: newly imported Buddhism gave the Taoism of Dark-Enigma Learning an institutional setting and a form of actual practice.

In the official Ch'an legend, Bodhidharma brought Ch'an from India more or less fully formed around 500 C.E., but his teaching is clearly built from the traditional Taoist conceptual framework, a fact revealed most simply in the way he depends on terms and concepts central to that Taoist system. In fact, Ch'an's origins are found a century or two earlier when Buddhist artist-intellectuals began melding Buddhism and Dark-Enigma Learning, which was broadly influential among artist-intellectuals at the time. In this process, they gave first form to most of the foundational elements of Ch'an that we will encounter in the following chapters. First among these, perhaps, is meditation.

The full transliteration of *dhyana* was *Ch'an-na,* 禪那. Of the many possible graphs that could have been chosen to transliterate *dhyana,* these would have been chosen for their Chinese meanings. 那 enriches meditative experience with its meanings "tranquility" and "that," as in the immediacy of consciousness ("that") in "tranquil" meditative experience. But 那 was dropped in normal usage, leaving 禪, a graph in which we can already begin to see the rich earthly and cosmological depths of Ch'an, for its pictographic etymology returns us to Taoist cosmology. And indeed, although it was the aspect of newly imported Buddhism most important to the development of Ch'an, *dhyana* meditation was reconceived according to China's native Taoist framework.

28

The 禪 graph divides into two elements: 礻 (示 in its full form) on the left, and 單 on the right. 示 derives from 川 and the more ancient oracle-bone form 示. This image shows heaven as the line above, with three streams of light emanating earthward from the three types of heavenly bodies: sun, moon, and stars. These three sources of light were considered bright distillations, or embryonic origins, of ch'i, the breath-force that pulses through the Cosmos as both matter and energy simultaneously—the dynamic interaction of its two dimensions, yin and yang, giving form and life to the ten thousand things and driving their perpetual transformations. It's remarkable how contemporary this ancient Chinese account of reality feels—for although the terminology is different (and the moon is only secondarily a light/energy source), this ancient Chinese description of reality is basically the same as our current scientific account. In this contemporary account that we take for granted, rarely feeling how wondrous and even strange it actually is, stars are in fact the "embryonic origins" of reality. For in their explosive deaths, stars create the chemical composition of matter. And in their blazing life, they provide the energy that drives earth's web of life-processes.

The common meaning of 示 was simply "altar," suggesting a spiritual space in which one can be in the presence of those celestial ch'i-sources. And indeed, if we were at a Ch'an monastery in ancient China, we would have experienced meditation as such a space, infused with those cosmological dimensions. It was also a practice of scientific observation, close empirical attention to the nature of consciousness ("seeing original-nature") and its movements. As such, it was the most essential part of the Ch'an adventure, Ch'an's primary method of awakening understood as "seeing original-nature."

29

In bare philosophical outline, meditation begins with the practice of sitting quietly, attending to the rise and fall of breath, and watching thoughts similarly appear and disappear in a field of silent emptiness. From this attention to thought's movement comes meditation's first revelation: that we are not, as a matter of observable fact, our thoughts and memories. That is, we are not that center of identity we assume ourselves to be in our day-to-day lives, that identity-center defining us as fundamentally separate from the empirical Cosmos. Instead, we are an empty awareness that can watch identity rehearsing itself in thoughts and memories relentlessly coming and going. Suddenly, and in a radical way, Ch'an's demolition of concepts and assumptions has begun. And it continues as meditation practice deepens.

With experience, the movement of thought during meditation slows enough that we notice each thought emerging from a kind of emptiness, evolving through its transformations, and finally disappearing back into that emptiness. Here, already, a new Taoist dimension is added to Buddhist *dhyana* meditation. *Dhyana* meditation, the conventional Buddhist form that came to China, cultivates consciousness as a selfless and empty state of "non-dualist" tranquility. Etymologically, *dhyana* means something like "to fix the mind upon," hence meditation as fixing the mind upon emptiness and tranquility. This aspect of meditation was hardly unknown in ancient China, appearing for instance in this passage from the *Chuang Tzu*:

You've heard of using wings to fly, but have you heard of using no-wings to fly? You've heard of using knowing to know, but have you heard of using no-knowing to know?

Gaze into that cloistered calm, that chamber of emptiness where light is born. To rest in stillness is great good

30

fortune. If we don't rest there, we keep racing around even when we're sitting quietly. Follow sight and sound deep inside, and keep the knowing mind outside.

But this must be seen in the Taoist context, as one aspect of meditative experience. And here at this stage in Ch'an meditation, we already find the Indian *dhyana* idea of meditation transformed by that context. We have moved beyond *dhyana*'s nirvana-tranquility and deep among Ch'an's cosmological and ontological roots in Taoism, inhabiting a generative origin moment/place in the form of "that chamber of emptiness where light is born."

In Ch'an, the process of thoughts appearing and disappearing manifests Taoism's generative cosmology, reveals it there within the mind. And with this comes the realization that the cosmology of Absence and Presence defines consciousness too, where thoughts are forms of Presence emerging from and vanishing back into Absence, exactly as the ten thousand things of the empirical world do. That is, consciousness is part of the same cosmological tissue as the empirical world, with thoughts emerging from the same generative emptiness as the ten thousand things.

These ontological dimensions are suggested by the graph for *monastery*, where meditation took place: 寺. The pictographic elements of 寺 can be seen better in earlier forms such as 寺: a hand below (⇒: showing wrist with fingers and thumb) touching a seedling above (屮: showing stem and branches growing up from the ground). This seedling image suggests "earth" as the generative source, so the graph's full etymological meaning becomes something like "earth-altar," a spiritual place where one "touches the generative."

Eventually the stream of thought falls silent in meditation,

31

and we inhabit empty consciousness free of the identity-center. That is, we inhabit the most fundamental nature of consciousness, known in Ch'an parlance as *empty-mind* or *original-mind*: *original* being 本, image of a tree (木, from earlier forms like 朮 showing a trunk with branches spreading above and roots below) accentuated by a mark locating meaning in the roots. This appears to be the tranquil emptiness of *dhyana* meditation, an emptiness in which mind is a mirror reflecting through perception the world with perfect clarity. But Ch'an meditation reveals that original-mind/mirror to be nothing other than Absence, generative source of both thought and the ten thousand things, for it is also the source from which thoughts emerge. And indeed, a fuller definition of 本 is something like "original source-tissue": hence, "original source-tissue mind."

Sangha-Fundament (Seng Chao) and Way-Born (Tao Sheng) were the most important Buddhist intellectuals involved in the amalgamation of imported *dhyana* Buddhism and Dark-Enigma Learning. But perhaps the most concise and influential was Hsieh Ling-yün (385–433), a giant in the poetic tradition who was a very serious proto-Ch'an practitioner. Hsieh wrote a short essay entitled "Regarding the Source Ancestral," described as an account of Way-Born's teaching and apparently the earliest surviving Ch'an text, in part because it advocates the quintessential Ch'an doctrine of enlightenment as instantaneous and complete. This essay indicates that Hsieh had a profound grasp of Way-Born's ideas and confirms that he had probably undergone a kind of Ch'an awakening himself. In it, Hsieh dismisses the traditional Buddhist doctrine of gradual enlightenment because "the tranquil mirror, all mystery and shadow, cannot include partial stages." And from this comes a description of meditation's fundamental outline that takes

32

a decidedly Taoist form: "become Absence and mirror the whole..."

Though we will see it reappear and develop in a host of ways, Ch'an deconstruction is already complete here in Hsieh's essay, and all the elements of awakening are in play. For we see as a matter of immediate observational experience the awakening suggested by Lao Tzu when he said: "if you aren't free of yourself / how will you ever become yourself." In this, already, we come to the foundational shift in awareness that is crucial to Ch'an awakening as "seeing original-nature": the experience of oneself not as a center of identity inside its envelope of thought and memory, but as an empty mirror, the contents of which is wholly the world it faces. And more: "original-nature" as nothing less than Tao or Absence, the generative existence-tissue that is the wordless Cosmos whole. Indeed, Seventh Patriarch Spirit-Lightning Gather (Shen Hui)* described awakening as simply "seeing Absence" (見無),[2] a variation on the Ch'an term we have seen for awakening: "seeing original-nature."

At these cosmological levels, Ch'an meditation is anticipated in Lao Tzu's *Tao Te Ching*, where much of the text describes meditative awareness, sometimes quite directly, as in: "Inhabit the furthest peripheries of emptiness / and abide in the tranquil center" or "sitting still in Way's company." And indeed, the Taoist cosmological dimensions of this "seeing original-nature" awakening are reflected in the graph for

---

* Spirit-Lightning Gather was Prajna-Able's dharma-heir and the person most responsible for creating the image of Prajna-Able as the seminal Sixth Patriarch. Hence, in terms of the development of Ch'an thought, it appears Spirit-Lightning Gather himself articulated many of the seminal ideas attributed to Prajna-Able.

33

Ch'an itself: 禪. As we have seen, 禪 depicts in its left element (礻: 示 in its full form) those cosmological sources of *ch'i* radiating down as a sacred altar-space. The right-hand half of 禪 is 單, an element meaning "individual" or "alone," a sense complemented by older meanings like "simple, great, entirely, exhaustively." Together, these elements describe the fundamental experience of Ch'an meditation: "alone simply and exhaustively *with* the Cosmos." With deeper meditation, this becomes "alone simply and exhaustively *as* the Cosmos," and finally: "the Cosmos alone simply and exhaustively with itself."

Breath

MEDITATION IS THE HEART OF CH'AN PRAC-
tice, and meditation begins with the breath:
sitting with the breath, attending to the breath. Breath helps
settle thought and quiet mind. But in Ch'an, breath is much
more. Life in, life out: breath reveals the entire conceptual
framework that shapes Ch'an. Each breath arises from nothing
and vanishes back into nothing, the essential movement of Tao:
inhale and exhale, sound and silence, full and empty, life and
death. Breath moves always at that generative origin-moment/
place. And so, attending to breath, like attending to thought,
reveals how utterly we belong to that cosmological/ontological
process of Tao.

The two ideograms of this chapter's title both mean "breath,"
each in a quite different way, though they are often combined
for richer expressiveness. In an early form, the top element of
息 (自) looked like 甴 or 㠯, which appears to render a kind
of emergence out of a generative space (generative emergence
a reasonable assumption because it is the fundamental structure of things in Taoist thought). And in its ancient oracle-bone
form, that emergence appears to come from two side-by-side

35

spaces that must represent lungs, and through an opening that must be a mouth. Artistically, it's a beautiful image: 𣎴, which becomes an equally beautiful concept: "breath-emergent."

The other word for breath is more expansive in its implications: 氣 (ch'i), which as we have seen (p. 25) describes the Cosmos as a single generative tissue breathing through its perpetual transformations. It seems 氣 was originally a veritable picture of sky's dynamic forces, which are driven by the sun's heat. Although the ancient oracle-bone forms are unknown, other early forms of 氣 suggest the graph originally contained the image of vapor 气 rising under the influence of heat. This heat appears as sun (portrayed in oracle-bone script as: ⊘) in 昛, or as flame 火 (from the oracle-bone image 𤆪) in 熹. Hence, ch'i in its most quintessential visible form: sky-ch'i, that living emptiness that we breathe in and out.

If we search the archaeology of mind, trace the etymologies of words describing mental states and processes back toward their origins, we find that they all came into the mental realm from the empirical. That is, they originally referred to images from the observable universe—things or processes or physical behavior. The human mind slowly created itself from those images through a complex process of metaphoric transference, thereby weaving the structures of identity from the empirical Cosmos. Our Western concepts such as spirit or psyche find their etymological origins in wind or breath. And as we have just seen, something very similar seems true in Chinese. Meditation, empty-mind attention to breath, essentially returns us to those primal levels of consciousness where the sense of consciousness or mind was being formed, for at those depths there is no distinction between breath and mind. At these originary metaphoric levels where consciousness shaped itself, the unity of mind and breath becomes apparent, and attending to

36

breath returns us to that place. This suggests a deeper dimension to the connection between breath and mind, for breath is that very sky taken inside us physically, while empty consciousness is that sky taken inside us mentally.

And indeed, the bottom half of the 息 graph (心) is *mind*, suggesting that primal unity of breath-emergence and mind. This is doubly interesting because 自 itself in fact means "self" (not surprising as it is breath that gives life), so the graph 息 associates breath and self/mind. The mysterious unity of breath and mind becomes immediately apparent in *ch'i*, for if we could trace consciousness back to its origins in the primeval word-hoard, back beyond the metaphoric constructions of subjectivity with its intentionality and reason, all the way back to some primal self-awareness of the opening of consciousness with its life and movement, we would no doubt find its empirical origin in the emptiness of dynamic living sky with its ever-changing breezes and humidity, temperature and weather and bottomless blue distances. And that leads us back to the cosmological dimensions of the *Ch'an* ("meditation") graph, showing three streams of light emanating earthward from the three types of heavenly bodies seen as bright distillations, or embryonic origins, of *ch'i*. How remarkable that those vast cosmological dimensions open so intimately in meditative breath-emergent mind!

37

心

Mind

MIND IN CH'AN PARLANCE REFERS MOST often to consciousness emptied of all contents. But Ch'an also uses *mind* in the common sense of the word, as the center of language and thought and memory, the mental apparatus of identity. This is necessary in order to describe the goal of Ch'an practice, which is to replace *mind* as the identity-center with *mind* as consciousness emptied of all contents. So understanding this core region of Ch'an thought and practice must begin with the common sense of *mind*; and in the Taoist/Ch'an framework, this mind is fundamentally different from the mind we in the modern West take for granted.

There was no sense in that framework of mind as a transcendental entity such as the West's "spirit" or "soul" that is ontologically separate from the world around it. Chinese has words that translate as "spirit" or "soul," but "spirit" was considered a particular condensation of *ch'i* breath-energy, and was therefore comprised of *ch'i*'s two aspects: the *yin* spirit (魄), which dispersed into the earth at death, and the *yang* spirit (魂), which dispersed into the heavens at death. In either case, they were more like energy fields that dissolve away soon after death. This more primal sense of spirit is reflected in the etymology for the graph meaning "spirit" more generally: 神, which depicts on the left that image we have seen of *ch'i* energy descending from sun, moon, and stars; and on the right, a streak of lightning slicing through sky. Hence: the sense of intense and brilliant energy in a sky-space.

In addition, there was no fundamental distinction between heart and mind: 心 (*hsin*) connotes all that we think of in the two concepts together. In fact, the ideogram is a stylized version of the earlier 心, which is an image of the heart muscle, with its chambers at the locus of veins and arteries. This integration of mental and emotional realms allows Ch'an's empty-mind dwelling as "the Cosmos alone simply and exhaustively with itself" to be not just a spiritual or intellectual experience, but also a rich emotional experience.

An even more dramatic expansion of our conventional sense of identity-center *mind* is distilled in the root concept 意 (*i*). Containing the pictographic element for "(heart-)mind" (心), 意 has a range of meanings: "intentionality," "desire," "meaning," "insight," "thought," "intelligence," "mind" (the faculty of thought). The natural Western assumption would be that these meanings refer uniquely to human consciousness, but 意 is also often used philosophically in describing the nonhuman world, as the "intentionality/desire/intelligence" that shapes the ongoing cosmological process of change and transformation. Each particular thing, at its very origin, has its own 意, as does the Cosmos as a whole. 意 can therefore be described as the "intentionality/intelligence/desire" infusing Tao/Absence and shaping its burgeoning forth into Presence, the ten thousand things of this Cosmos. It could also be described as the "intentionality," the inherent ordering capacity, shaping the creative force of *ch'i*.

39

This range of meaning links our human mind (intention/ thought) to the originary movements of the Cosmos, so translating/conceiving the term as *"ch'i*-thought" or *"ch'i*-mind" opens the cosmological context for the idea of an "intelligence" that infuses all existence, and of which human thought is but one manifestation. So, 意 is a capacity that human thought and emotion share with wild landscape and, indeed, the entire Cosmos, a reflection of the Chinese assumption that the human and nonhuman form a single tissue that "thinks" and "wants." Hence, mind not as a more or less transcendental identity-center separate from and looking out on reality—our assumption in the West—but as woven wholly into the ever-generative *ch'i*-tissue, into a living and "intelligent" Cosmos.[3]

Words

Taoist and Ch'an masters from the beginning insisted at every turn that words are the
fundamental impediment to deep insight. Words, thoughts,
ideas: they serve a practical function, an evolutionary purpose.
They intend to get us somewhere: to work toward understanding, solve a problem, make a plan, all in the project of navi-
gating the world and surviving. Ch'an is useless: it wants to
go nowhere else, solve no problem. It wants no words and no
understanding. Not least, no understanding of Ch'an itself.

Ch'an teaching always deploys words to tease mind past
the realm of words. And Ch'an's two basic forms of practice—
meditation and sangha-case (koan: for which see p. 113 ff.)
training—are still more radical and direct strategies for dismantling that realm of words, thereby returning mind to its
original empty nature. But to understand wholly what this meant
in the original Ch'an, we must understand how words and language functioned in ancient China—for as with mind, they
functioned very differently than they do in the modern West.

In the modern West, we experience language in a mimetic
sense—as a transcendental realm that looks out on the world,

using words to represent it, to point at it. Language is the medium of thought, and its transcendental nature creates the illusion of mind as a transcendental identity-center. This assumes language did not evolve out of natural process, that language as a transcendental spirit-realm somehow came into existence independently of natural process. And indeed, language is described this way in the Judeo-Christian myth that still shapes Western assumptions in fundamental ways, for the language of humans was God's language at the beginning, so it oddly predates the physical universe. When language functions in this mimetic sense, it embodies an absolute separation between the identity-center ("soul") and reality. And that separation defines the most fundamental level of experience.

Rather than a timeless and changeless transcendental realm pointing out at reality, classical Chinese functions non-mimetically. Each word is associated with the thing it names not because of a mimetic pointing at the thing from a kind of outside, but because it shares that thing's embryonic source. Tao itself is the physical Cosmos seen as an undifferentiated source-tissue. This source-tissue is only divided into individual things when we name them. Those names emerge from the undifferentiated tissue exactly like the things they name, and they emerge at exactly the same moment: it is only when the word *mountain* appears that the mountain itself appears as an independent entity in the field of existence. The mountain exists prior to the naming, of course, but it isn't separated out conceptually as an independent entity. And it is there at this origin-moment/place that meaning happens in classical Chinese: word and thing coming into existence together at the same moment, and therefore sharing the same root.

This non-mimetic function is embodied in the pictographic nature of classical Chinese, wherein words are most fundamentally images of things. Rather than alphabetic marks that are distant and arbitrary signs referring to reality from a seemingly transcendental outside, pictographic Chinese words operate without the dualistic divide between empirical reality and a transcendental realm of language. In their pictographic form, they share with things their very forms. And in the cultural myth, this language emerged quite literally from the earth—for it was invented by the first human, who emerged from a mountain as half-human and half-dragon (mythical incarnation of Tao and the awesome force of change itself). In this, language retains its roots in the primitive, where it was oral and free of the metaphysics introduced by writing. Indeed, the graph meaning "words" is a picture of speech, words rising out of a mouth: 言, the base element at the heart of virtually all graphs having to do with language.

Non-mimetic language assumes the primal generative cosmology of Taoism. It is only in this experience of reality as an all-encompassing emergent present that non-mimetic language can exist, for each word needs to operate at that very origin-moment/place, word and thing emerging into existence simultaneously. And so, we find that language too inhabits the generative origin-moment/place. We have already seen this in meditation, which reveals thought/words emerging in consciousness from the generative emptiness of Absence. This integration of language and empirical reality is described in another framework: the ontology/cosmology of Absence and Presence. Language is simply one aspect of Presence emerging from the pregnant emptiness of Absence. It has the same ontological status as the ten thousand things, and therefore belongs wholly to the cosmological process of Tao.

43

This ontological rooting of language is reinforced by the assumption that language is a natural pattern, one among the countless patterns that emerge as Tao unfurls into the great transformation of things. It was a manifestation of "ch'i-thought/mind" (意), that "intelligence" infusing all existence and shaping Tao's burgeoning forth into the ten thousand things (p. 39 f.). Even in its most carefully composed written form, language was considered an organic part of Tao's unfolding. The word for literary works (and by extension culture and civilization) is 文, the elemental meaning of which is "the moving patterns Tao reveals as it emerges into empirical reality": veins in stone, ripples in water, patterns of stars and seasonal transformations. And writing was assumed to be another of those patterns. According to *Literary [文] Mind and the Carving of Dragons* (c. 500 C.E.), a widely influential work on language and literature, words are the "pattern [文] of Tao." Rather than a medium that conscribes consciousness within an isolate identity-center, writing was instead a return to origins or a majestic expression of Tao, especially in its most distilled form as poetry. And this sense of written language suffuses Chinese culture (and therefore Ch'an practice). Indeed, 文 is the radical for a broad range of words having to do with writing, literature, and culture.

Seeing into the primal non-mimetic nature of classical Chinese reveals what is invisible to us in our own language. At the foundational ontological levels where Ch'an practice operates, English in fact functions in the same non-mimetic way as classical Chinese, but our deep cultural assumptions preclude us from experiencing it that way. Especially important for Ch'an practice is the idea that Tao's undifferentiated source-tissue is only divided into individual things when we name them, and that this naming isolates us from the

44

immediate world of things. So, one can only dwell as integral to Tao prior to the differentiation and separation that naming creates, an idea that permeates Ch'an, as we will see. Hence, the Taoist/Ch'an teaching that understanding can only be wordless, a principle stated in countless ways across the tradition. Yellow-Bitterroot Mountain (Huang Po), to take one of countless examples, says

> Anything said is not dharma and is not original source-tissue mind. In this, you begin to understand dharma transmitted mind-to-mind.[4]

And so, when Ch'an practice returns us to empty-mind without words and logical categories, it returns us to dwell as integral to that undifferentiated existence-tissue.

Words are the medium of the identity-center, and with that identity-center comes a separation between self and everything else. In the West, this separation is metaphysical because of the transcendental nature of the mimetic language-realm, and because of mythologies in which the self is a "soul," that transcendental spirit-center. In classical Chinese, the separation exists, but there is no metaphysical dimension. Language is not a transcendental realm, and neither is the identity-center. There is a separation, the overcoming of which is the focus of Ch'an practice, but that practice is quite different because there is no metaphysical dimension involved.

Taoism and Ch'an recognize that only outside of words and ideas, only prior to the naming that creates an identity-center separate from the ten thousand things, is it possible to dwell as integral to Tao, that generative source-tissue unfurling the great transformation of things. And it is that primordial place to which Ch'an meditation and sangha-case (koan) practice return us. But as we will see, once it familiarizes us with that primordial place, Ch'an practice stops trying to erase language-structured thought/identity. Instead, as part of "seeing original-nature," it enables us to inhabit thought/identity as integral to Tao and the selfless simultaneity of its unfolding. Mind and Cosmos are a single tissue, the identity-center emerging together with language and perception and the ten thousand things at that origin-moment/place. And indeed, it is inhabiting that origin selflessly that is Ch'an's final intent.

II

Absence

O F TAO'S TWO ELEMENTAL PRINCIPLES, Absence and Presence, Absence is the more fundamental. It is nearly synonymous with Tao, but emphasizes Tao as the undifferentiated generative source-tissue. Absence's generative and dynamic nature is reflected in its etymological origin as the pictograph of a woman dancing, her swirling movements enhanced by fox tails streaming out from her hands: 無. Cultivation of this Absence as the fundamental nature of consciousness was described as central to Ch'an practice/insight over and over across the tradition.[5]

At the very beginning of Ch'an's development, Hsieh Ling-yün's "Regarding the Source Ancestral" (p. 32) describes the essence of practice in terms of Absence: "become Absence and mirror the whole." *Absence* positively permeates the widely read and chanted *Mind Sutra* (aka *Heart Sutra*, 649 C.E.), as in this incantatory passage:

And so, in emptiness this beautiful world of things is
   Absence,
perceptions Absence, thoughts, actions, distinctions,

Absence eyes and ears, nose and tongue, self and
  meaning and *ch'i*-mind itself,
Absence this beautiful dharma-world,
its color and sound, smell and taste and touch,
Absence the world of sight
and even the world of *ch'i*-mind, its meanings and
  distinctions,
Absence Absence-wisdom
and Absence Absence-wisdom extinguished,
Absence old-age unto death
and Absence old-age unto death extinguished.[6]

Nearly two centuries later, Yellow-Bitterroot Mountain stated it directly:

Mind is of itself Absence-mind, is indeed Absence-mind Absence. If you nurture Absence-mind mind, mind never becomes Presence.[7]

As we have seen, Spirit-Lightning Gather said that the essence of awakened *prajna*-wisdom is simply "seeing Absence" (見無), thereby equating Absence with original-nature in Bodhidharma's original formulation: "seeing original-nature" (見性). And nearing the end of Ch'an's golden age of development, the Sung Dynasty teacher No-Gate Prajna-Clear described the "gateway of our ancestral patriarchs" as "the simplest of things, a single word: *Absence.*"[8] And as we will see, No-Gate made Absence the organizing center of his *No-Gate Gateway,* one of the greatest and most influential works of Ch'an literature.

It is both confusing and revealing that Absence is virtually synonymous with "emptiness" (空 or 虛) in Taoist and Ch'an texts. Our language and intellectual assumptions have trained

50

us to interpret such terms as a kind of nonmaterial metaphysical realm in contrast to the material realm of Presence, and "emptiness" generally operates that way in other forms of Buddhism. We interpret Absence and Presence as a dualistic pair, in which Presence is the physical universe and Absence is a kind of metaphysical void from which the ten thousand things of physical reality emerge. But artist-intellectuals in ancient China, whether poets or Ch'an masters, would not have recognized any metaphysical dimensions in this dualism, for they were all thoroughgoing empiricists. And in the empirical reality of the Cosmos, there is no metaphysical womb somewhere, no transcendental pool of pregnant emptiness.

Absence is emptiness only in the sense that it is empty of particular forms, only Absence in the sense that it is the absence of particular forms. In normal everyday use, *Absence* (無) means something like "(there is) not," and *Presence* (有) means "(there) is." So the concepts of Absence and Presence might almost be translated as "form-less" and "form-ful," for they are just two different ways of seeing the ever-generative tissue of reality. Absence is all existence seen as one undifferentiated tissue (reality, as we have seen, prior to our names), while Presence is that same tissue seen in its differentiated forms, the ten thousand things (reality differentiated by our names). And it should also be emphasized that both terms, *Absence* and *Presence*, are primarily verbal in Chinese: hence, that tissue of reality is seen as verbal, rather than the static nominal: a tissue that is alive and in motion.

Because it is generative by nature, magically generative, the tissue of existence is perennially shaping itself into the individual forms we know—the ten thousand things—and reshaping itself into other forms: the natural process of change, of life and death, transformation and rebirth. From this it follows that

51

Absence and Presence are not two separate realms of reality, but are instead a single tissue all origin through and through. This unity of Absence and Presence appears in the first chapter of the *Tao Te Ching*, the first clear description of the deep cosmological/ontological levels of Taoist philosophy:

In perennial Absence you see mystery,
and in perennial Presence you see appearance.
Though the two are one and the same,
once they arise, they differ in name.

As is so often the case with Lao Tzu, there is no distinction here between subjective and objective realms. It sounds like he's talking about objective reality, but it blurs into the realm of consciousness. And of course this is perfectly accurate—for as we've seen, it is naming that creates distinctions in the tissue of reality.

And so, Tao (Way) might best be understood as a single dynamic and generative "existence-tissue." This explains why the landscape elements in Chinese paintings also seem infused with Absence, why they are drawn as outlines containing the same pale color that renders emptiness throughout the painting. It's because the concepts of Absence and Presence are simply an approach to the fundamental nature of things, and in the end they are the same: Presence grows out of and returns to Absence and is therefore always a manifestation of it.

This unity will prove fundamental to Ch'an understanding, as we've already glimpsed in the *Mind Sutra* above. Or to take another anticipatory example, the widely influential "Fact-Mind Inscription" (generally translated with formulations like "Faith/Trust/Belief in Mind") by the Third Patriarch Mirror-Wisdom Sangha-Jewel (Seng Ts'an: 529–613) says directly:

Presence is exactly Absence,
and Absence exactly Presence.[9]

And Yellow-Bitterroot Mountain says

if you stop seeing in terms of Absence and Presence, you
will see dharma itself.[10]

無 has another more common meaning: the simple grammatical function word *no/not*. This double-meaning is play-
fully exploited in a central way through the entire Taoist/Ch'an
tradition. It figures in a number of key philosophical terms, but
it also functions as a kind of poetic strategy, as in the *Mind
Sutra* above (p. 49). And to take another especially prominent
example, it is central to the great sangha-case (koan) collection
No-Gate Gateway. This wordplay begins with the author's
tellingly paradoxical name, No-Gate/Absence-Gate (無門),
which is repeated in the book's title: *No-Gate/Absence-Gate
Gateway*. But perhaps most influential of many instances, this
wordplay is also the key to *No-Gate Gateway*'s first sangha-
case, which became widely considered the foundation of
sangha-case practice because it forces a direct encounter with
Absence and Buddha-nature:

A monk asked Master Visitation-Land: "A dog too has
Buddha-nature, no [無]?"
"No/Absence [無]," Visitation-Land replied.

Rendered here in a translation that mimics the original's
grammatical structure, this might seem a simple if puzzling
exchange. But No-Gate's comment to this sangha-case claims
that Visitation-Land's 無 is the "No-Gate Gateway" to Ch'an's
ancestral essence. In the American tradition of Zen, this 無 is
taken as a blank denial of meaning-making, which is registered

53

by letting the word remain untranslated, an inexplicable nothing: *mu* (the Japanese pronunciation for 無, which in Chinese is pronounced *wu*). Hence, something like:

A monk asked Master Visitation-Land: "Does a dog have Buddha-nature?"
"*Mu*," Visitation-Land replied.

This leaves the sangha-case at a generic level of "Zen perplexity." But when 無 is seen in its native conceptual context, No-Gate's claim begins to reveal itself in its full richness, for here it means not just utter negation, but also "Absence." Not just the denial of meaning-making, but also the generative ontological ground.

The monk's question about the dog could have been formulated differently in the original Chinese. The stark affirm-deny construction, a standard form in Chinese, was clearly chosen because it allows the monk's question to end with the same 無 that immediately becomes the master's reply. In the question, 無 would appear to be nothing more than a grammatical function word coming at the end of a sentence ("A dog too has Buddha-nature, no?"), which makes Visitation-Land's 無 breathtaking, for it suddenly deepens that insignificant 無 all the way to the source of everything: Absence, that formless and pregnant tissue from which all things arise.

This seems a large part of how the sangha-case works, and it leads us to realize that "has/have," the seemingly unremarkable word occurring earlier in the question, is in fact Presence (有), which has a double meaning almost the exact opposite of 無: "is/has" and "Presence." With this, another version of the monk's question echoes behind the literal: "A dog too Presences Buddha-nature, or Absence?" Once the question is invested with its cosmological depth, Visitation-Land's 無

dramatically ends thought, leaving empty-mind free to "wander all heaven and earth in a single stride," as No-Gate says in a poem immediately preceding this sangha-case.[11]

Absence itself represents the most profound and all-encompassing of sangha-cases, teasing the mind past ideas and explanations at fundamental cosmological levels. As we have seen, No-Gate described the "gateway of our ancestral patriarchs" as "the simplest of things, a single word: *Absence.*" And when a monk asks about Buddha-nature, the essence of consciousness, our original nature, Visitation-Land mysteriously replies: "Absence." So Visitation-Land's response to the question about dog and Buddha-nature is multifaceted. It is an expression or description of his mind at that moment, implying the monk should emulate his empty-mind rather than struggle for some abstract understanding. And it is an enigmatic comment on the question, an enactment of Buddha-nature, which thereby attempts to shut down meaning-making. Hence, a challenge directed at the monk, insisting that giving up thought and explanation is the only way to fathom Absence— empty-mind in its most profound sense. So the sangha-case asks us to ponder Absence, to inhabit our original-nature as nothing other than that generative emptiness at the heart of the Cosmos. Not simply the tranquil silence of *dhyana* meditation, it is something much deeper: that dark vastness beyond word and thought, origin of all creation and all destruction.

55

Empty-Mind

C H'AN MEDITATION ALLOWS US TO SEE through language and thought and memory, the mental apparatus of identity, to that empty awareness that is the original-nature of consciousness: free of the identity-center, and free of that separation between self and Cosmos. This original-nature is also known in Ch'an parlance as *empty-mind* (空心), consciousness in its original undifferentiated state, emptied of all contents. Intense and formalized cultivation of empty-mind in meditation is *dhyana*'s primary contribution to Ch'an. But while it is true that Ch'an ends conceptual thought in empty-mind, it does so within the conceptual framework of Taoist ontology/cosmology. As we have seen, that framework was taken for granted by original Ch'an practitioners, and Ch'an practice was about making it real in immediate experience. Indeed, that was the breakthrough of awakening. Key to the cultivation of this awakening is understanding how the nirvana-tranquility of *dhyana*'s empty-mind (which in Indian Buddhism often involves metaphysical notions of rebirth and the end of rebirth) is transformed by

56

Taoism's conceptual framework into Ch'an's quite different sense of empty-mind.

空 itself also means quite simply "sky," that vast empty space alive and dynamic with movement. Hence, empty-mind as "sky-mind." Again, Ch'an's return to the most primal levels of consciousness—for as we have seen, sky must be the primordial metaphoric origin of consciousness. 空心 is therefore quite literally the "original-nature" of consciousness. That dynamic sky appears again in a synonym for 空 in the Taoist/ Ch'an syllabary: 虛, or 虗 in its early form. 虗 is pictographically constructed of a sky whose life-energy is especially dramatic. The first of its two elements is a pair of mountain peaks: 丠. And in the space above and surrounding those peaks, there is a tiger: 虍, deriving from early images like 𧇂. Together, these two elements give 虗 an etymological meaning of something like: "mountain tiger-sky." Hence, "empty-mind" becomes: "mountain tiger-sky mind."

Empty-mind is the most fundamental and original nature of consciousness; and so, Ch'an confusingly calls it simply *mind.* This is in fact the most common meaning of *mind* in the Ch'an literature: consciousness emptied of all contents. This mind is the central concern of the great Yellow-Bitterroot Mountain, who uses both of the terms for "empty/sky" when he describes mind as "radiant purity like the emptiness of empty sky (空虛)." And he continues, saying mind is

like the emptiness of empty sky—no confusion, no ruin. Empty sky where the vast sun wheels around, blazing down from the four heavens. When it rises, illuminating everything throughout all beneath heaven, the empty-sky emptiness is not illuminated. And when it sets, darkening everything throughout all beneath heaven, empty-sky

57

emptiness is not darkened. Illumination and darkness alternate, but the emptiness of empty sky, its vast and expansive nature, never changes.

And further, as we discover in meditation: empty-mind is nothing other than the generative tissue dynamic and alive, reflected in the fact that 空 is synonymous in the Ch'an literature with 無 (Absence). Indeed, there is a common variation of 空心 ("empty-mind"): 無心 ("no/Absence-mind), where 無 replaces 空 as a virtual synonym. Here we begin to see how the philosophically rich double meaning of 無 is exploited in key Taoist/Ch'an concepts, for here *no-mind*, an apparently exact synonym for empty-mind, is also *Absence-mind*, consciousness in its original-nature as that dynamic and generative ontological tissue, which is nothing other than Tao itself. Hence, Yellow-Bitterroot Mountain's statement that we saw above meaning "mind is of itself Absence-mind" (p. 50) is simultaneously read "mind is of itself no-mind." Returning empty-mind again to its roots in empty sky, the deeply influential Purport Dark-Enigma* (died 866) said "mind-dharma is no-form [無形], and it opens clear through the ten distances of time and space." Here again, we find the double meaning of 無, and reading Purport's 無 as "Absence" rather than "no" gives "mind-dharma is Absence-form, and it opens clear through the ten distances of time and space."

In addition to equating Absence with original empty-mind nature, Spirit-Lightning Gather described his own Buddha-nature mind as the source of all things. Solar-South Prajna-

---

* Purport Dark-Enigma (義玄) was commonly known as Lin Chi (臨濟: Jap. Rinzai) because he was abbot of a monastery at Lin Chi, which means "River-Crossing Overlook."

58

Loyal, another of the Sixth Patriarch's dharma-heirs, said that the one way to awakening is to "abide in the mind-source." And Yellow- Bitterroot Mountain calls empty-mind the "source-tissue."

Absence and the generative source are synonymous with Tao. And indeed, empty-mind as Tao is a steady refrain through the Ch'an tradition. It is already suggested by Chuang Tzu, who recommends a practice of "fasting" that he describes this way:

> But the primal spirit is empty: it's simply that which awaits things. Way is emptiness merged, and emptiness is the mind's fast.

Perhaps the most famous teaching of the very influential Patriarch Sudden-Horse Way-Entire (Ma Tsu: 709–788) is: "Ordinary mind is Tao/Way." This *Tao* refers to the Ch'an "way" of practice leading to awakening; but as normal in Ch'an, it also and more fundamentally refers to Lao Tzu's cosmological/ontological Tao. And here we see there is no real difference between the two, for mind is Ch'an's "way" to awakening exactly because it is nothing other than the generative emptiness of Tao.

Way-Entire's descendent, the illustrious Purport Dark-Enigma (Lin Chi), quotes Way-Entire's line and says it represents the essence of Ch'an. And we find the line again in an exchange between two more of Ch'an's most prominent masters: Visitation-Land (who appears as a master in the 無 [not/Absence] sangha-case on p. 53 ff.) and his teacher Wellspring-South Mountain. The student Visitation-Land's awakening comes in an encounter with Wellspring-South Mountain that begins:

59

Visitation-Land asked Wellspring-South Mountain: "What is the Way?"

"Ordinary mind is Way," answered Master Wellspring.

And it's true, empty-mind is always open within us as the structure of everyday perception. Hence, the Ch'an insight that we are always already enlightened—that there is no need for Ch'an practice as a search for understanding/awakening—as in the full explanation Master Wellspring-South Mountain offered when Visitation-Land reached awakening:

Visitation-Land asked Wellspring-South Mountain: "What is Way?"

"Ordinary mind is Way," answered Master Wellspring.

"Still, it's something I can set out toward, isn't it?"

"To set out is to be distant from."

"But if I don't set out, how will I arrive at an understanding of Way?"

"Way isn't something you can understand, and it isn't something you can not understand. Understanding is delusion, and not understanding is pure forgetfulness.

"If you truly comprehend this Way that never sets out for somewhere else, if you enter into it absolutely, you realize it's exactly like the vast expanses of this universe, all generative emptiness you can see through into boundless clarity."

And in Purport Dark-Enigma's masterful distillation: "Primal-unity mind is Absence [無], so anywhere you are is liberation."[12]

Here again is Ch'an's conceptual framework as fundamentally Taoist in nature: mind as Absence, mind as Tao. Hence, mind woven wholly into the Cosmos at the deepest ontological level. This identification of empty-mind and Absence may be Ch'an's most fundamental transformation of *Dhyana* Buddhism. And if we pursue the nature of empty-mind deeper into Taoist/Ch'an ontology and further from *dhyana* nirvana-tranquility, it gets more mysterious still. For it returns us to that originary moment where words and things emerge into existence together. As we have seen, it is only when names impose distinctions on the undifferentiated existence-tissue that those distinctions come into existence as the ten thousand differentiated things. Words and things emerge into existence at that same origin-moment/place. And that is also the moment when the first structures/distinctions defining identity emerge into existence. As mind is slowly emptied of words through meditation, it becomes more and more undifferentiated; and at the same time, the world in our experience becomes more and more undifferentiated. Hence, Cosmos and mind are simultaneously undifferentiated. Here is empty-mind as the gateway to awakening: once mind is undifferentiated, once the last scrap of identity is extinguished, we inhabit that origin-moment/place, dwelling wholly integral to Cosmos as the generative tissue of Tao.

This is the mind that Ch'an teachers famously transmit outside of words and ideas, teachings and texts. And indeed, it is itself the greatest of teachers, an idea that appears already in the *Chuang Tzu*:

If you follow the realized mind you've happened into, making it your teacher, how could you be without a teacher? You don't need to understand the realm of change: when mind turns to itself, you've found your teacher. Even a numbskull has mind for a teacher.

Among Ch'an teachers, Sixth Patriarch Prajna-Able says:

61

To recognize in your own mind the consummate teacher: that is liberation. . . . To realize in sight's clarity-absolute the consummate teacher: that is the one awakening in which you know Buddha completely. When the insight of your own original-nature and mind-ground sees with deep illumination, penetrating the sage radiance of inner and outer, you recognize your own original source-tissue mind. And to recognize your source-tissue mind—that is liberation itself.

And Yellow-Bitterroot Mountain recounts Prajna-Able echoing the Bodhidharma poem we saw above (p. 13):

When Bodhidharma came from the West, he simply pointed at mind: it's in mind itself that you *see original-nature* [見性: Bodhidharma's definition of "awakening"] and become Buddha, not in words and talk.

Empty-mind is about much more than simple tranquility or attentiveness, essential as they may be. It is, instead, everyday ordinary mind operating at Tao's generative origin-moment/place, which the Dark-Enigma Learning master Kuo Hsiang described as the "hinge of Tao" where our "movements range free" because we move as the Cosmos (Tao) itself unfurling inexhaustibly through its boundless transformations.

Mirror

EMPTY-MIND, MOUNTAIN TIGER-SKY MIND, Absence-mind: free of the self-enclosed mental machinery of the identity-center, mind is liberated into an opening of awareness that functions like a mirror looking out on the world. Ch'an practice focused on cultivating mirror-deep perception as a spiritual act. This awakening to consciousness as a mirror is transformative because thought isolates us in the subjective, awareness focused on mental processes rather than the world of perceptual experience. When thought stops, that moment of awakening, we are wholly present in life as a moment-by-moment experience of incandescent perceptual immediacy. Indeed, it represents the central transformation Ch'an offers an individual: to be immediately and wholly present in one's life, mirror-deep eyes gazing out with the clarity of an empty awakened mind. That is, in a sense, everything: rather than living in the self-enclosed distraction of our mental machinery, to inhabit our lives wholly moment-by-moment in the absolute clarity and incandescence of things.

Empty mirror-deep mind is a recurring motif in Ch'an literature, and the crux in one of that literature's most legendary

63

moments. Narrating a time when Sixth Patriarch Prajna-Able was a student, the *Platform Sutra of the Sixth Patriarch* recounts how the Fifth Patriarch asked students to write a poem that would reveal the level of their awakening, promising that whoever revealed the most awakened insight would become his dharma-heir. The students all deferred to the head-monk, who wrote a poem on the monastery wall that described meditative practice as a discipline involving mind as a brilliant mirror:

Body is the Bodhi-awakening tree
where mind stands like a brilliant

mirror. Polish it clean day after day,
never let the least dust gather there.

The poem demonstrates the head-monk's awakening because in mirror-deep perception we experience ourselves not as a center of identity, but as the ten thousand things that fill empty mirror-deep mind. This may be the beginning and end of Ch'an: the identity-center replaced by the wordless thusness of things in and of themselves. No ideas, no stories, no certainties, no questions and no answers, no seeking—just empty-mind become the elemental thusness of reality experienced as sheer wonder and mystery. Indeed, in *Ch'an-na*, 禪那—the full Chinese transliteration of the *dhyana* ("meditation")—那's meanings "tranquility" and "that" suggest the immediacy of things in mirror-deep perception. And there is no end of Ch'an stories revealing this thusness as the whole of Ch'an, as in these examples from the koan collection *Blue-Cliff Record*:

Whenever a question was posed, Master Million-Million simply raised one finger. [chapter 19]

64

A monk asked Vast-Dragon: This self and this beautiful world of things: they crumble into ruins. What is the strong and enduring dharma-self?"

"Mountain flowers opening like brocade," replied Dragon, "streamwater deep and clear as blue-indigo." [chapter 82]

A monk asked Master Wisdom-Gate: "What is the potency of awakened *prajna*-wisdom?"

"An oyster holding the radiant moon in its mouth," replied Gate.

"And what is the expression of awakened *prajna*-wisdom?" asked the monk.

"A rabbit pregnant and full-bellied."* [chapter 90]

Utterly simple, utterly themselves, and utterly sufficient: the ten thousand things, understood at full cosmological/ontological depths were known as *tzu-jan* (自然). Literally meaning "self-so" or "the of-itself," *tzu-jan* is a near synonym for *Tao* or *ch'i*. But it is best translated as "occurrence appearing of itself," for it emphasizes the particularity and self-sufficiency, the *thisness*, of the ten thousand things burgeoning forth spontaneously from the generative source (Presence from Absence), each according to its own nature, independent and self-sufficient, each dying and returning to the process of change, only to reappear in another self generating form.[13]

The salient pictographic feature of the second graph in

---

* *Potency* (體) and *expression* (用) together represent an important pair of foundational cosmological/ontological concepts in Chinese philosophy. *Potency* refers to the inherent potentiality or nature of things that gives shape to their particular *expression* or "instantiation/manifestation" in the world. See also p. 106.

65

tzu-jan (然) is *fire*: ⺗, abbreviated form of 火, which is a simplified version of earlier fire images such as this oracle-bone rendering: ⺕. The first word in *tzu-jan* (自) is an element we have already seen (p. 35 ff.) meaning something like "breath-emergent." Hence, *tzu-jan* and the ten thousand things as "breath-emergent thusness ablaze with itself." Yellow-Bitterroot Mountain spoke of *tzu-jan* as "the great wisdom." And indeed, how could this realm of *tzu-jan* not be the greatest of teachers, the primary engine of awakening as it breathes blazing through mirror-deep mind, the wordless thusness of things, their sheer presence resounding through consciousness? The moon, for instance, whose chill light seems almost the image of empty-mind awakening. In the record of Visitation-Land's awakening, it simply says his mind was the clear moon. And it was little different for the great Ch'an poet Cold Mountain. Cold Mountain took his name from the mountain where he lived, and often in the poems he is indistinguishable from the mountain. Indeed, it is said that he ended by simply vanishing into a cliff there. In life, he lived near a Ch'an monastery, ridiculing the monks who so earnestly practiced without realizing they were already awakened, and he too described awakening in terms of the moon:

Under vast arrays of stars, dazzling depths of night,
I light a lone lamp among cliffs. The moon hasn't set.

It's the unpolished jewel. Incandescence round and full,
it hangs there in blackest-azure skies, my very mind.

Tzu-jan as teacher, then, is the ten thousand things mirrored in all their clarity, without the names we give them, names that distance them from us. Indeed, to see things, to mirror them

66

perfectly, requires that we forget the names of things, forget names and ideas that package reality in our human constructions. Then things seen go mirror-deep inside consciousness and simply vanish there, eluding us perfectly as they become us, no self anywhere. In Ch'an, this is to inhabit that generative origin-moment/place, for cultivating mirror-deep perception was not an attempt to hold on to tranquil moments: it was instead an embrace of *tzu-jan*'s movement as oneself, things appearing and vanishing inside us. This practice was there from the beginning, in Chuang Tzu:

Live empty, perfectly empty.

Sage masters always employ mind like a pure mirror: welcome nothing, refuse nothing,

reflect everything, hold nothing.

Hsieh Ling-yün's seminal "Regarding the Source Ancestral" calls empty-mind "the tranquil mirror, all mystery and shadow," and adds that for enlightenment one must "become Absence and mirror the whole." Hence, as we have seen, mind not as an empty spirit-mirror, as our Western assumptions might assume, but as that generative Absence, a living generative tissue that is somehow mirror-deep with awareness. And so, Hsieh's empty-mind "Absence" as "all mystery and shadow" transforms the experience of oneself so that consciousness takes on the vast cosmological depths of Absence itself. The perceptual clarity of empty mirror mind becomes *Absence perceiving*—or in modern Western terms, the wild Cosmos perceiving itself. A fact Prajna-Able suggests when he calls empty mirror-mind the "original source-tissue face . . . that's been gazing out since the very beginning of things."

Presence, then, is a near synonym for *tzu-jan*. The standard graph for *Presence*, 有, evolved out of earlier, more clearly pictographic forms, such as 㝆 (in which the two pictorial elements are inverted left to right), portraying a hand covering the moon to create an eclipse, the very image of "mystery and shadow." There's no explanation for how this graph came to mean "Presence," but what could be more overwhelmingly mysterious than Presence, than the fact that it exists, that there is something rather than nothing? All day long, year in and year out, that Presence fills our mirror-deep minds, whispering all its silence through us, replacing meaning/thought with the elemental beauty of meaninglessness, the clarity of the ten thousand things. And it's easy not to notice. Here again we find Ch'an insight originating in close attention to the nature of everyday experience, revealing that we are always already enlightened: in the immediate moment-by-moment field of mirror-consciousness, this vast opening that we are, Presence dwarfs the identity-center.

In the *Platform Sutra*, the head-monk's idea of polishing the mirror (p. 64) was radically revised by the Sixth Patriarch, who rewrote the head monk's poem to reveal his own awakening:

Mind is the Bodhi-awakening tree,
body where a brilliant mirror stands,

original source-tissue mirror such
pure-clarity—what could dust stain?

Prajna-Able's was a radically more profound insight than the head monk's. The head monk's proposition enshrines a fatal separation between the mirror and some self that is polishing it. And by focusing practice on polishing the mirror, a

68

way of describing the *dhyana* meditation that in the context of Indian Buddhism was redolent with notions of karmic purification, he assumes awakening to be the perfection of this mirror-consciousness as a tranquil space separate from the world's onslaught of change and transformation.

Prajna-Able's radical revision evades both of those errors. He realizes mind is always already a mirror. No matter how confused a state we are in, there is absolutely no separation between us and the mirror. Hence, we are always wholly what is passing through the mirror, wholly *tzu-jan* occurrence. Missing in the head monk's poem is the Taoist understanding that came to shape Ch'an. This mirrored perception is never the stillness of a single perception for long. Instead, the content of mirror-deep consciousness is in constant movement and transformation. And so, in mirror-deep perception we live integral to Tao's wilderness cosmology at the deepest ontological levels. We live wide-open at that generative origin-moment/place, that "hinge of Tao."

Prajna-Able's revision also proposes that consciousness is always already perfectly empty and enlightened, that there is no need for a disciplined perfecting of consciousness, the discipline of *dhyana* meditation. This is his "original source-tissue face . . . that's been gazing out since the very beginning of things." And with it, Prajna-Able dismantles Ch'an practice itself, for as long as that empty-mind is the subject of practice or explanation/understanding, it remains out there as a kind of goal. Similarly, not long after Prajna-Able, the poet Tu Mu (803–853) dismantled the mirror metaphor and even subjectivity itself in his own way, while also returning to that primordial "sky-mind," when he described himself gazing "into a flawless mirror of sky." Once again, Ch'an masters as a wrecking-crew demolishing any and all explanatory constructs.

69

It is only when we end practice and explanation that we can inhabit empty-mind in and of itself: the "sudden awakening" of Ch'an. Hence, Prajna-Able prefaced his poem with this explanation:

If you don't fathom original source-tissue mind, studying Dharma won't get you anywhere. But if you fathom mind, you see original-nature—then you're awakened to the vastness of $ch'i\text{-}mind$.[14]

And so, there is nothing to practice because we are always already enlightened, always already Absence somehow open to the world. Or again, in more contemporary scientific terms, we are in our original-nature the Cosmos aware of itself.

It is quite literally true, of course. The Cosmos evolved suns and eventually, in the third generation of suns, our planet. And here, the Cosmos evolved life forms with image-forming eyes like ours, through which it looks out at itself: very ancient, if not quite "gazing out since the very beginning of things." And so, in a scientific sense, empty mirror-mind is indeed always already awakened, always already the very nature of everyday experience. Free of the identity-center, that empty mirror-mind is the same no matter whose eyes are looking out. Which is why Ch'an texts often say that in awakening we meet Buddha and all the patriarchs face to face. Or more: that we become them, that we ourselves become Buddha. For Buddha is most essentially the empty-mind he was awakened to when meditating under the bodhi tree.

This identity of practitioner and Buddha was also true at deep cosmological/ontological levels, for empty mirror-mind is consciousness as that undifferentiated source-tissue. Call it empty-mind or Absence-mind, original-nature or mirror-mind—this is self-identity in its most majestic form, as

70

tzu-jan occurrence, that *blazing breath-emergent thusness.* And whether we are in the midst of vast rivers-and-mountains landscapes or at home moving through our everyday routine, this empty mirror-mind is always already 禪 (Ch'an): "the Cosmos alone simply and exhaustively with itself."

山水

Rivers-and-Mountains

THE MOST MAGISTERIAL MANIFESTATION OF *tzu-jan*'s blazing breath-emergent thusness is *rivers-and-mountains*, the Chinese term normally translated as "landscape," as in "landscape painting" or "landscape poetry." The cultivation of Ch'an mirror-mind is most essentially landscape-practice, because rivers-and-mountains landscape is where Taoist/Ch'an cosmology is most consumingly available to immediate experience. Rivers-and-mountains is where *ch'i*'s breath-force takes on its grandest living manifestation, rivers being *yin* and mountains *yang*. And mountains are where heaven and earth, embodiment of *yang* and *yin* on the most cosmic scale, mingle most dramatically: earth tipping up and churning into heaven, heaven seething down to mingle all windblown mist and sky breathing through earth.

Or conceived in another framework: mountains are where Presence burgeons from Absence in its most majestic forms, a cosmology rendered in countless landscape paintings, where Absence appears as vast empty spaces from which Presence emerges in the form of landscape (p. 23). Ancient artist-intellectuals saw in the wild forms of mountain landscape the

72

very workings of the Taoist/Ch'an Cosmos: not as abstraction, but at the intimate level of immediate experience. And because it is where existence reveals its most dramatically cosmological dimensions, immediate mirror-deep experience of mountain landscape opens consciousness most fully to the depths of those dimensions.

This explains the centrality of landscape in Chinese culture and Ch'an practice: indeed, the abiding spiritual aspiration of China's artist-intellectuals was to dwell as integral to rivers-and-mountains landscape. The cultivation of this dwelling took many forms, all of which recognized rivers-and-mountains landscape as the open door to realization. Ancient artist-intellectuals lived whenever possible as recluses in the mountains, wandered there where that cosmological process could be experienced in the most immediate possible way. The arts were considered ways to cultivate that dwelling: poetry being most essentially rivers-and-mountains poetry, painting most essentially rivers-and-mountains painting. And that dwelling was also the central concern of Ch'an practice.

Ch'an's beginnings can be traced to around the fourth century C.E., when there was a resurgence and deepening of Taoist thought (Dark-Enigma Learning) together with the beginning of landscape's centrality for China's artist-intellectuals, most notably when China's mature mainstream poetic tradition emerged in the form of rivers-and mountains poetry invented by two epochal poets: T'ao Ch'ien and Hsieh Ling-yün (author of "Regarding the Source Ancestral," a seminal text in Ch'an). The reason for this is no doubt the mirror-deep clarity of empty mirror-mind that Buddhist meditation so resolutely cultivated. And in fact, the original meanings of the *Ch'an* ideogram, before it was chosen to translate the Sanskrit *dhyana* ("meditation"), were "altar" and "sacrifice to rivers-and-mountains."

73

Hence, meditation as a place where one honors or celebrates rivers-and-mountains. In addition, Ch'an monasteries were typically located in remote mountains (those in cities surrounded themselves with the domesticated landscapes of gardens), and Ch'an masters leading those monasteries generally took the names of local mountains as their own because they so deeply identified with mountain landscape: Hundred-Elder Mountain, Yellow-Bitterroot Mountain, Cloud-Gate Mountain, Heaven-Dragon Mountain, Wind-Source Mountain, River-Act Mountain, Buddha-Land Mountain, Cloud-Lucent Mountain, Doubt-Shrine Mountain, Fathom Mountain, Moon-Shrine Mountain, and indeed: Mirror-Sight Mountain.

Ch'an as landscape-practice involved erasing two structures of thought, both generally familiar to us by now, that separate consciousness from landscape. First is the fact that thought inevitably distracts attention from the perceptual moment, isolating us inside our mental world and separating us from immediate experience of that cosmology. Only by cultivating empty mirror-mind can one attend to the magisterial cosmology of rivers-and-mountains wholly. The second structure is perhaps less obvious, though it is closely related to the first. Thought is always *about* something outside itself, creating the impression that we are somehow fundamentally separate from the Cosmos. That impression is reinforced by the apparent structure of perception, in which the illusory center of identity that thought constructs makes perception seem always to be *of* something else. And for ancient China's artist-intellectuals, nothing could better carry us outside of our self-enclosed world of thought than the dramatic realm of mountains and rivers.

Free of thought and the center of identity, the opening of consciousness becomes a bottomless mirror opening landscape through us and allowing no distinction between inside and

74

outside. This is the awakening that Ch'an landscape practice cultivates, as in this poem by Li Po (701–762) describing a kind of landscape meditation:

Reverence-Pavilion Mountain, Sitting Alone

Birds have vanished into deep skies.
A last cloud drifts away, all idleness.

Inexhaustible, this mountain and I
gaze at each other, it alone remaining.

It is whole: empty awareness and this expansive presence of existence. It is a single tissue. And to dwell there without all of the words and explanations, empty-mind mirroring rivers-and-mountains landscape with perfect clarity, that is complete and whole: identity become landscape filling eye and mind, become indeed the existence-tissue vast and deep, everything and everywhere.

But there's more. For Ch'an, rivers-and-mountains landscape offers a way into the "inner-pattern" (理), a root concept in Chinese philosophy that recurs often in the Ch'an literature. *Inner-pattern* originally referred to the network of veins and markings within a precious piece of jade, and that is an image of its philosophical meaning: the inherent ordering pattern that shapes the unfurling of Tao or *ch'i* in the cosmological/ontological process of change, a concept little different than *ch'i*-thought/mind (意), which as we have seen (p. 39 f.) refers to the "intentionality/desire/intelligence" infusing Tao and shaping the burgeoning forth of Absence into Presence. Inner-pattern therefore weaves Absence and Presence into a single boundless tissue. It explains the wondrous fact that matter is so exquisitely organized into the intricate forms of this rivers-and-mountains world—forests and oceans,

75

snakes and orcas, poppies and humans—that those forms somehow appear and evolve in and of themselves and for no apparent reason. And cast against the possibility of a pattern-less and therefore chaotic evolution of things, as it always was in the Chinese mind, that pattern is sheer miracle.[15]

Concepts at these depths blur, especially in this intermingling of Taoist and Buddhist thought; and in the hands of various ancient Chinese writers, *inner-pattern* appears virtually synonymous with a host of other root concepts: Tao, Absence, and *tzu-jan*, for example, or Buddha and awakened *prajna*-wisdom. In any case, inner-pattern entails a vision of the Cosmos as an undifferentiated whole, and Ch'an awakening means dwelling as integral to that undifferentiated whole. In terms of immediate experience, this means empty-mind awareness of things existing and moving according to their own inherent nature or "inner-pattern." Water, for instance, moving in its own particular way outside of all our utilitarian preconceptions of it that arise from our practical need for it as something essential to life, moving as a mysterious and elemental planetary liquid. Or consciousness (not at all unlike water, as the ancient Chinese recognized), its fluid movement between thought and emotion, perception and silence. The goal of Ch'an landscape practice, then, is to dwell as empty mirror-mind consciousness participating in that inner-pattern, and finally to move as integral to the inner-pattern.

Inner-pattern appears in the early Taoist texts *I Ching* and *Chuang Tzu*. It is further developed in Dark-Enigma Learning philosophy, where Kuo Hsiang described the inner-pattern as

> this ground from which the ten thousand things are born. It includes those things, for origins can only include progeny, and it carries them back to the origin-tissue.

Dark-Enigma Learning was the philosophical inheritance of Hsieh Ling-yün, the seminal rivers-and-mountains poet. And in his "Regarding the Source Ancestral" essay, Hsieh dismisses the traditional Buddhist doctrine of gradual awakening because "the tranquil mirror, all mystery and shadow, cannot include partial stages," then explains:

Become Absence and mirror the whole, then you're returned to the final and total enlightenment of inner-pattern understood clear through to the end.

Hsieh Ling-yün wrote "Regarding the Source Ancestral" when he was beginning to develop his rivers-and-mountains poetics. For him, one comes to this dwelling through *adoration* (賞), which denotes an aesthetic experience of the wild rivers-and-mountains realm "mirrored" as a single overwhelming whole—and that dwelling was tantamount to awakening. It is this aesthetic experience that Hsieh's poems try to evoke in the reader. Early in his epic "Dwelling in the Mountains," Hsieh speaks of "embracing . . . the inner-pattern's solitude" and "choosing the sacred beauty of occurrence coming of itself [*tzu-jan*]." The poem then unfurls a torrent of grandiose language, headlong movement, and shifting perspective, giving it an elemental power that captures the dynamic spirit and inner rhythms that infuse the numinous realm of rivers-and-mountains. And reading it requires that we participate in his mirror-whole dwelling:

6

Here where I live,
lakes on the left, rivers on the right,
you leave islands, follow shores back

77

to mountains out front, ridges behind.
Looming east and toppling aside west,

they harbor ebb and flow of breath,
arch across and snake beyond, devious

churning and roiling into distances,
clifftop ridgelines hewn flat and true.

12

Far off to the south are
peaks like Pine-Needle and Nest-Hen,
Halcyon-Knoll and Brimmed-Stone,

Harrow and Spire Ridges faced together,
Elder and Eye-Loft cleaving summits.

When you go deep, following a winding river to its source,
you're soon bewildered, wandering a place beyond knowing:

cragged peaks towering above stay lost in confusions of mist,
and depths sunken away far below surge and swell in a blur.

Inner-pattern is a major presence in the Ch'an literature,
where it is already central to practice and awakening in the
recorded teachings of Bodhidharma, the First Patriarch of
Chinese Ch'an. Bodhidharma calls it one of the two paths for
"entering Tao," says that through meditation and the rejection
of written teachings we can "reach deep accord with the inner-
pattern," a place of such cosmological/ontological depth that
it is where "the distinction between Absence and Presence
arises." And a few paragraphs further on he simply says that by
"abiding in inner-pattern" we can reach "awakening all clarity
absolute."[16]

78

Patriarch Sudden-Horse Way-Entire (Ma Tsu) says that in the awakening of a Buddha, "you penetrate through both inner-pattern and this world that it shapes." When one of Purport Dark-Enigma's students attained enlightenment, the student is described as having realized inner-pattern. Purport himself said that awakening is attained "only by practicing in accordance with inner-pattern" (of course, he went on to dismantle the proposition). And in *No Gate Gateway*, awakening is described as seeing "the inner-pattern of Way":

Mirror-Sight Mountain hungrily questioned Dragon-Lake into the night. Finally, Lake said: "The night is deep. You should have left by now."

Mountain bowed in homage, raised the blinds, and left. But seeing it was dark out, he stepped back in and said: "It's pitchblack out there!"

Lake lit a paper-lantern candle and offered it to him. Then, just as Mountain reached out to take it, Lake blew it out. At this, Mountain was suddenly awakened. He bowed reverently, and Lake asked: "You just saw the inner-pattern of Way. Tell me, what is it?"[17]

Hsieh Ling-yün began a Ch'an sense of landscape practice in the amalgam of his poetry and the understanding revealed in his Ch'an essay. Then, as Ch'an developed in the centuries that followed, its empty mirror-mind transformed Chinese poetry, grounding it in the clarity of rivers-and-mountains images. This imagistic clarity became the fabric from which poetry was made, poetry that was widely considered a form of Ch'an practice and teaching. And in a culture where there is no distinction between heart and mind, it makes sense. Perception clarified by meditation until it is empty-mind mirroring the ten thousand things, mirroring rivers-and-mountains landscape:

79

it isn't just an intellectual or spiritual experience, it is also an emotional experience, an experience of the *heart*. That experience of the heart is presumably the purview of poetry, and indeed there is no end of such rivers-and-mountains poems in ancient China. A quintessential example is work by the great Wang Wei (701–761), a seminal figure in rivers-and-mountains poetry and painting (and whom we will see writing an influential memorial inscription for the Sixth Patriarch):

Magnolia Park

Autumn mountains gathering last light,
one bird follows another in flight away.

Shifting kingfisher-greens flash radiant
scatters. Evening mists: nowhere they are.

Or this especially pure imagistic poem by Tu Mu, who we saw (p. 69) dismantling the mirror metaphor:

Egrets

Robes of snow, crests of snow, and beaks of azure jade,
they fish in shadowy streams. Then startling up into

flight, they leave emerald mountains for lit distances.
Pear blossoms, a tree-full, tumble in the evening wind.

A rivers-and-mountains poetry of images weaves the identity-center into landscape as accurately as language can. It thereby renders a larger identity, an identity that is made of landscape. This is the heart of Ch'an as landscape-practice: in mirror-deep perception, earth's vast rivers-and-mountains landscape replaces thought and even identity itself with its breath-emergent blaze, revealing the unity of consciousness and landscape/Cosmos that was sage dwelling for Ch'an practitioners, and indeed for all artist-intellectuals in ancient China. It returns us to our most primal nature, that inner wilds where we are indeed the awakened landscape gazing out at itself.

In the end, Ch'an revered rivers-and-mountains landscape (much like empty-mind) as a great teacher. This is implicit as an assumption throughout the tradition, and we find it stated openly when Wang Wei mourns the death of his great predecessor in the lineage of imagistic Ch'an landscape poetry:

Mourning Meng Hao-jan

My dear friend nowhere in sight,
this Han River keeps flowing east.

Now, if I look for old masters here,
I find empty rivers-and-mountains.

And Visitation-Land states it directly:

A monk asked Master Visitation-Land: "What is my teacher?"

Visitation-Land replied: "Clouds rising out of mountains, streams entering valleys without a sound."

Dharma

THE CHINESE TRANSLITERATION FOR THE Sanskrit *dharma*, is 法. 法 originally meant "a river ford," derived from the etymological elements "water" and "to leave," hence dharma as a means of "crossing over" into awakening. That is its sense in the forms of Buddhism that arrived in China, which is no doubt why 法 was chosen to translate the Sanskrit *dharma*. But as Ch'an developed, that crossing over was recognized as always already happening in everyday moment-to-moment experience (another instance of Ch'an disassembling concepts), and that recognition entailed a radical transformation in the concept of dharma itself.

In common usage, 法 means "law." The first sense of the "law" in Ch'an is simply the teachings of the Ch'an tradition, the essential truths about reality and the essential principles that guide practice. But that initial meaning is quickly dismantled, because Ch'an's essential teaching resides outside of words and ideas. And that leads to the most fundamental meaning of *dharma*: the fundamental laws or patterns that govern the unfolding of Tao as it unfurls into the ten thousand things. With this, as we see over and over with Buddhist

82

terminology, *dharma* has been transformed into the native Chinese philosophical framework as a virtual synonym for *inner-pattern* or *ch'i-thought/mind*.

As we saw in Hsieh Ling-yün, inner-pattern in its cosmological manifestation is revealed most dramatically in rivers-and-mountains landscape. And indeed, landscape practice is the other principal way of knowing dharma, for it provides access to those cosmological dimensions. The common phrase "ten thousand dharmas" means all of the things and processes that make up the Cosmos. And so, *dharma* becomes virtually synonymous also with *tzu-jan, Tao, Absence, ch'i*, etc. Hence, the Buddhist concept of *dharma* was adapted to function at the deepest cosmological/ontological levels of the Taoist conceptual framework, where concepts blur together.

This radical transformation in the meaning of *dharma* clearly followed the model of *Tao*—for Tao's more straightforward meaning was "the way" in the sense of the teachings or principles that guided practice in various philosophical schools, and that meaning was expanded to become the cosmological/ontological concept. Further, dharma continues the demolition that began in early Taoist practice—for as with Tao that cannot be known in words, dharma is not the dharma of words, dharma-teaching not the dharma-teaching of ideas. And as we have seen for *Tao*, dharma is often equated with empty-mind itself, as in this passage from Yellow-Bitterroot Mountain:

This dharma is mind: outside of mind, there is no dharma. And this mind is dharma: outside of dharma, there is no mind.

Indeed, after equating dharma and mind, Yellow-Bitterroot Mountain continues (in a passage we have already seen) to equate both to Absence: "Mind is of itself Absence-mind, is

83

indeed Absence-mind Absence." So in Ch'an, dharma can be known through meditation where one can "see original-nature." In fact, Bodhidharma described dharma as "the inner-pattern of original-nature's purity."[18]

And so, dharma's wordless teaching resides in empty-mind, rivers-and-mountains landscape, the sheer thusness of every-day life. In the end, dharma is nothing other than the genera-tive existence-tissue of all birth and death and transformation. And as Patriarch Sudden-Horse Way-Entire says, dwelling as integral to that dharma is itself the liberation of awakening:

> The dharma of all things themselves, that is the Buddha-dharma. All those dharmas together are liberation, and that liberation is the existence-tissue itself all clarity absolute.

84

Buddha

BUDDHA REFERS MOST LITERALLY TO THE historical Shakyamuni Buddha, of course: the Buddha of Buddhism, the origin and center of it all. As such, Buddha was a prime target for the Ch'an wrecking-crew's project of dismantling ideas and certainties, for as long as we are captivated by the idea of Buddha and his teachings, as long as we try to understand them, we have not come to empty-mind immediacy of thusness. Hence, the only way to realize Buddha-mind is to erase Buddha and his teachings. And the only way to become Buddha is, famously, to kill Buddha. By now, erasing Buddha begins to look familiar. For as with Tao and Absence, Buddha is only realized without words and concepts (including especially the word and concept of *Buddha*). This demolition of Buddha is a recurrent theme in Ch'an literature and the practice it describes. On the one hand, Buddha is ridiculed, denied, and erased. And on the other, Buddha is described in paradoxical ways meant to break down conceptual thinking by deconstructing what appears to be the most essential project for conventional Buddhists: to understand Buddha and his teachings.

85

The question "What is Buddha" appears over and over in the Ch'an literature, as a foundational question asked of various masters, and the answers are wildly paradoxical and contradictory, as in these examples:

Flax. Three pounds.
Mountains are all around us here.
Dry shit-wipe stick!
You

Such answers intend to replace abstract ideas about Buddha and his teachings with strikingly immediate images of thusness and therefore empty-mind. Similarly, Patriarch Sudden-Horse Way-Entire, one of the most influential of all Ch'an masters, is asked this question numerous times. Once he answers: "This very mind is Buddha." Then another time, he responds: "Not mind, not Buddha," an answer that has several effects. First, it perfectly contradicts his first answer. And second, it erases Buddha and all he means to Buddhism, while at the same time simply dismantling the question itself.

Beyond using him as an element in storytelling, Ch'an is primarily interested in Shakyamuni at the deep level of his essential nature: that open space of consciousness he cultivated through meditation under the bodhi tree. So for Ch'an, *Buddha* is most essentially the "empty-mind" that remains once we finish asking what Buddha is, emphasized in the terms *Buddha-mind* and *Buddha-nature*, synonymous with *empty-mind* and *original-nature*. When Sudden-Horse Way-Entire says Buddha is "not mind," his intent is performative rather than descriptive: as so often in Ch'an, he is enacting insight, trying the open empty-mind as Buddha-nature in the questioners by dismantling their analytical thought. And to take a more direct example, the *Platform Sutra* gives a second

86

version of Prajna-Able's poem (p. 68) in which the "brilliant mirror" becomes "Buddha-nature":

Original source-tissue Bodhi-awakening
isn't a tree. Nowhere stands the brilliant

mirror. Buddha-nature perennially such
pure clarity—where could dust gather?

In his poetic distillation of Ch'an (p. 13), Bodhidharma described awakening as becoming Buddha: "seeing original nature, you become Buddha," and that "original-nature" is, of course, empty-mind. The second Patriarch put it simply and directly: "Mind is Buddha." And Yellow-Bitterroot Mountain said: "Buddha is originally mind, mind all emptiness empty." This insight was central throughout the tradition, where awakening to empty-mind as original-nature is often described as meeting Buddha and the patriarchs face-to-face, or as being indistinguishable from them. For in empty-mind, consciousness is without that center of identity that would distinguish us from Buddha. What remains is empty consciousness itself, the Cosmos looking out at itself, which is in itself the same gaze whoever and wherever the individual may be. This empty mirror-mind experience was also, for ancient Chinese artist-intellectuals, a way of communing absolutely with friends. It was a common activity for friends to gather and share mirror-deep perceptual experience: perhaps meditating together, perhaps sipping wine (which, not unlike meditation, eases the isolate ego-center away), and then gazing at mountain landscape or a rising moon. And that meant sharing something deeper even than the identities we think of as the subjects of love and friendship. This leads to a profound sense of sangha, sangha sharing rivers-and-mountains awakening.

87

The perceptual clarity of empty mirror-mind is the very nature of this Buddha-mind, and of course that Buddha-mind is open and mirror-deep always, however mundane and everyday our experience. This leads to the Ch'an insistence that we are always already Buddha, always already awakened. But the magisterial dimensions of rivers-and-mountains landscape opens that mirror-mind most dramatically. We have seen rivers-and-mountains as dharma, and here we have rivers-and-mountains as Buddha, as Ch'an teachers of the first order.

So at these deep levels, Buddha is also indistinguishable from dharma, as put concisely by the Second Patriarch: "Mind is Buddha. Mind is Dharma. Buddha and dharma: they aren't two separate things." This is one more instance of cosmological/ontological distinctions collapsing together, and revealing again the thusness of the ten thousand things as the true wordless teaching. For it is thusness that returns consciousness to empty-mind or Buddha-mind. And as rivers-and-mountains landscape is the most imposing manifestation of that thusness—call it *tzu-jan* or dharma—rivers-and-mountains are not just wordless teaching, they are Buddha. This becomes quite literal when Su Tung-p'o, the great Sung Dynasty poet and calligrapher, described mountain landscape as the Buddha's body in his enlightenment poem:

A murmuring stream is the tongue broad and unending,
and isn't a beautiful mountain the body pure and clear?

And finally, in the Ch'an collapse of cosmological/ontological distinctions, rivers-and-mountains landscape is, as we have seen, Tao in its most dramatic manifestation. Lord-Celestial and Heaven, divine objects of veneration in early China, were transmuted into Tao (p. 4 f.). And the same thing happened to Buddha: semi-divine object of veneration in Buddhism as it

88

arrived in China, Buddha too became Tao. For China's empiricist artist-intellectuals, reality seen whole was the only possible object of veneration: Tao, the great ongoing transformation of things.

Ch'an invests empty-mind with Taoist ontology/cosmology, making empty-mind indistinguishable from Tao or *tzu-jan* occurrence, Absence or *ch'i*—and so, *Buddha* becomes synonymous with those concepts too. Hence, *Buddha* is absorbed wholly into the Taoist cosmology, becoming another term used to describe the generative tissue at the source of all things in both the mental and physical realms—a fact revealed most succinctly in the term *Buddha-Way (Tao).* Or in the Chinese transliteration for *Tathagata,* a name for Buddha as the "thus-come" or "thus perfected one": "existence-tissue arrival" (如來). So, to become Buddha is to move as empty-mind at that generative origin-moment/place, as Yellow-Bitterroot Mountain suggests when he repeatedly calls empty-mind the "pure-clarity source-tissue Buddha of origins."

玄

Dark-Enigma

THE FOUNDATIONAL CONCEPTS WE HAVE BEEN tracing are Ch'an's way of orienting us, its approach to the core aspiration of enlightenment as "seeing original-nature." But once we are oriented, the next step is disorientation. And this, as we have seen, is the Ch'an wrecking-crew's most fundamental methodology: the dismantling of our conceptual orientation. That means razing the entire Taoist/Ch'an ontology/cosmology that we have slowly come to understand through those foundational concepts, and that appears to be a system of answers. This understanding has brought us into a remarkable place, a remarkable way of knowing/experiencing consciousness and Cosmos and their interrelation. But in the end, Ch'an liberation resides outside words and ideas, answers and certainties and stories. And so, it requires that we dismantle them. As we will see, that is exactly what meditation and sangha-case (koan) training do: cultivate understanding outside of words and ideas and stories.

But this dismantling of concepts operates in the teachings too, the words and ideas, as in this moment from Bodhidharma that begins with the "original-nature" that is seen in awakening, then blurs a string of heavy-duty concepts together:

Original-nature is simply mind itself. Mind is Buddha. Buddha Tao. And Tao is Ch'an.

Tao, Absence and Presence, tzu-jan (occurrence appearing of itself), ch'i (breath-force), rivers-and-mountains landscape, empty-mind, no-mind, Absence-mind, mirror-mind, original source-tissue mind, original-nature, original source-tissue face, Buddha, dharma, inner-pattern, ch'i-thought/mind, existence-tissue, Buddha-nature, Buddha-mind, prajna-wisdom: these are the terms that describe the contours of Taoist/Ch'an ontology/cosmology. Each term emphasizes a different aspect of that ontology/cosmology, but by now it is becoming clear that in the end they all blur into a single concept, a single linguistic darkness, and this darkness is itself the cosmological/ontological ground: that undifferentiated and generative tissue of the Cosmos seen as a single organic whole.

There was a name for this mysterious darkness: *dark-enigma* (玄), which is an image of two silk-cocoons suspended into a vat of purple-black dye, visible in the early version 𤇢— where the horizontal element is either a rack from which the cocoons are suspended, or the water's surface. Lao Tzu, with his sly humor, invented *dark-enigma* for the impossible task of naming existence-tissue as it is in and of itself before any names, before Absence and Presence give birth to one another, and before all those other words and concepts and distinctions we use to approach the fundamental nature of existence. For as we have seen, that undifferentiated existence-tissue is only differentiated when we begin to name it: individual things arising simultaneously with their names. And so, in

91

the naming of words and ideas, that originary source tissue is unavoidably lost. Hence, dark-enigma as an opening into the wordless understanding that is essential to Ch'an.[19] It is described perfectly in the first chapter of the *Tao Te Ching*, which ends with its mysterious darkness:

In perennial Absence you see mystery,
and in perennial Presence you see appearance.
Though the two are one and the same,
once they arise, they differ in name.

One and the same they're called *dark-enigma*,
dark-enigma deep within dark-enigma,

gateway of all mystery.

And dark-enigma appears in the name of the philosophical school that emphasized the ontological depths of Taoism and combined with newly-arrived Buddhism to form Ch'an (p. 27 f.): Dark-Enigma Learning. There is a similar strategy in the Ch'an term *emptiness empty* (空虛), which we have seen used a number of times (not least as a description of sky). Like *dark-enigma*, it is a way of saying emptiness emptied of conceptual content, before concepts including the concept of emptiness. But *dark-enigma* itself recurs at revealing moments in Ch'an texts. Sangha-Fundament, the Buddhist intellectual instrumental in combining Dark-Enigma Learning philosophy with imported Buddhism to create Ch'an, wrote in 410 that

a sage's mastery of emptiness perfectly Absence-alive: that is the perspective of *prajna*-wisdom's dark-enigma mirror.

And this passage from the Third Patriarch's important "Fact-Mind Inscription" (commonly translated as "Faith/

92

Trust/Belief in Mind") frames dark-enigma explicitly in the Taoist/Ch'an cosmological/ontological framework, with its fundamental concepts of dharma, emptiness, *tzu-jan* (occurrence appearing of itself):

When mind is undivided, the ten thousand
dharmas become primal unity existence-tissue,

primal unity existence-tissue all dark-enigma
in which you forget even emptiness itself.

Fathoming the ten thousand dharmas whole,
you return to occurrence appearing of itself.[20]

Dark-enigma was taken as a dharma name by many Ch'an figures, including Purport Dark-Enigma (Lin Chi: Jap. Rinzai). He spoke of dark-enigma in terms similar to Lao Tzu: "to grasp things and use them, but without names arising: that is called dark-enigma."[21] And he taught that once awakened to Buddha-nature, we "ride the surge of circumstances," "a person of Tao dependent upon nothing," and he calls this the "dark-enigma of all Buddhas."[22] Indeed, he said "Buddha-dharma is dark-enigma in quiet mystery,"[23] where *quiet mystery* (幽) operates in a particular way at the deep cosmological/ontological level of dark-enigma, for its philosophical meaning is "things ever so slightly on the undifferentiated (not-yet-emergent) side of the ongoing origin-moment where the ten thousand things (Presence) emerge from Absence: forms not quite come into existence as differentiated entities or just barely vanished back into the undifferentiated ground." And dark-enigma remained current in Ch'an thought: five-hundred years later, to take one example, *No-Gate Gateway* describes master Buddha-Land Mountain saying to his students:

Open wild origins and penetrate the depths of dark-enigma: that's the only way to see your original-nature.[24]

Dark-enigma is a return to consciousness prior to language and the distinction between consciousness and empirical reality, at a level where they are a single whole—vast and deep, everything and everywhere. Lao Tzu speaks of mind as a "dark-enigma mirror" and asks: "Can you polish the dark-enigma mirror / to a clarity beyond stain?" Hence, like Prajna-Able's mirror (p. 68), empty-mind as a mirror prior to all concepts and distinctions (including the concept of *mirror*). As soon as it is conceptualized, named even with this first name, *dark-enigma*, the mirror's immediacy and wholeness are lost.

Dark-enigma cannot be portrayed directly because it is exactly the generative existence-tissue prior to the distinctions of forms, of names, or even of consciousness separate from things. But in its blur of all the foundational ideas, dark-enigma points the way past language and the knowable to wordless awakening. Dark-enigma can only be known in immediate experience, but it is possible to suggest the nature of this experience—as Lao Tzu does when he describes meditation as cultivating "dark-enigma union," or No-Gate Prajna-Clear when he says that we must "penetrate the depths of dark-enigma: that's the only way to see your original-nature" (remembering the Ch'an description of awakening as "seeing original-nature"). And even at the beginning with Kuo Hsiang, the proto-Ch'an Dark-Enigma Learning philosopher, this dark-enigma mind is described as liberation:

no-mind inhabits the mystery of things. . . . This is the importance of being at the hinge of Tao. There, you can know dark-enigma's extent. There, your movements range free.[25]

94

III

Absence-Action

SAGE WISDOM IN ANCIENT CHINA MEANT UNDER-standing the deep nature of consciousness and Cosmos, how they are woven together into a single fabric, and how to inhabit that weave as an organic part of Tao's generative cosmological/ontological process. As we have seen, this habitation is the intent of meditation practice with its empty mirror-mind that erases the distinction between inner and outer. Its other primary form in Ch'an was *wu-wei* (無為), which means "not acting," in the sense of acting without the identity-center self, or acting with an empty and therefore wild mind. This selfless action is the movement of *tzu-jan* occurrence, so *wu-wei* means action integral to *tzu-jan's* spontaneous burgeoning forth. And further, it is action at origins—for the *wu* in *wu-wei* is 無 with its philosophically revealing double meaning: "not/Absence." So, in addition to "not-acting," *wu-wei* means "Absence-acting," or perhaps "enacting Absence." Here, *wu-wei* action is action directly from, or indeed, *as* the generative ontological source: as Absence burgeoning forth into Presence. To borrow Kuo Hsiang's terms: in *wu-wei* our "movements range free" because we

97

move at the "hinge of Tao." And in the blurring of concepts at these cosmological/ontological depths, action as Absence is action as Tao, *ch'i*, Buddha, dharma, inner-pattern, and all the rest. Or in contemporary terms, it is to act as the Cosmos itself moving with selfless spontaneity.[26]

Wu-wei is a foundational assumption shaping ancient Chinese intellectual culture; and as Ch'an is integral to that culture, *wu-wei* is also a foundational assumption shaping Ch'an practice. Its meaning is therefore taken for granted, like all of the fundamental Taoist/Ch'an concepts, and so is rarely discussed in the Ch'an literature. But as we will see in the next two chapters, *wu-wei* is the central principle defining Ch'an's core practices of meditation and sangha-case (koan) training.

When Bodhidharma asserts that through meditation we can "reach deep accord with the inner-pattern," where "the distinction between Absence and Presence arises" (p. 78), he continues to say that there we "master the tranquility of *wu-wei*."[27] And when he says that by "abiding in inner-pattern" we can attain "awakening all clarity absolute," (p. 78) he continues to explain how in that awakening "a serene mind is all *wu-wei*."[28] In his "Fact-Mind Inscription," the Third Patriarch puts it simply: "Sage-masters are Absence-action [*wu-wei*]."[29] When Spirit-Lightning Gather asked the great Wang Wei (p. 80) to write a memorial inscription for the Sixth Patriarch, Wang wrote that even practicing *dhyana* meditation for *kalpas* (cosmic cycles of 4,320,000 years) "can't compare with a life of *wu-wei*." A serious Ch'an practitioner and seminal master of Ch'an rivers-and-mountains poetry and painting, Wang was widely connected in intellectual and Ch'an circles, and such inscriptions were meant to be memorial praise that would charm people in those circles, so his claim no

98

doubt echoed Prajna-Able's own teaching and also a broad assumption within the Ch'an community.

Other examples of *wu-wei*'s currency in Ch'an thought include Yellow-Bitterroot Mountain saying:

> The ancients had sharp minds all wild bounty. Hearing even a single word, they gave up all learning. And so they were called those who gave up learning and mastered the *wu-wei* idleness of Tao.

And Patriarch Sudden-Horse Way-Entire brought the Ch'an project of dismantling all concepts and certainties to *wu-wei* too, saying that awakening also means "never dwelling in Absence-action [*wu-wei*]."

Again, this is Ch'an revealed as integral to the broader Chinese cultural complex, for *wu-wei* was a central concept in the seminal teachings of the Taoist sages Lao Tzu and Chuang Tzu; and it was thereafter a spiritual practice that all artist-intellectuals in ancient China pursued in their daily lives and in their artistic practices. The essence of this *wu-wei* living is to simply do exactly what we are doing, to do it wholly and selflessly, spontaneously and without any separation from it. Here, Ch'an immediacy goes beyond just empty-mind mirroring to comprise our everyday actions: whether it's taking a walk or cooking dinner. And this applies even more to the long slow course of life as a whole—moving as *wu-wei* through success and failure, flourishing and attrition, loss and finally death. To inhabit life with this immediacy is to be wholly a part of Tao's great transformation, for the movement of our life is always already *tzu-jan* occurrence. So, to inhabit it wholly like this is to live as *tzu-jan*, as Tao, as the Cosmos itself. This is Ch'an's promise of a way to live one's life in its largest dimensions.

One manifestation of cultivating *wu-wei* in daily life is a practice ancient artist-intellectuals called "idleness." As we have just seen, Yellow-Bitterroot Mountain speaks of ancient sages mastering "the *wu-wei* idleness of Tao." And the great poet Tu Fu (712–770) says "It is here, in idleness, I am real." Etymologically, the character for idleness connotes "profound serenity and quietness," its pictographic elements rendering a tree standing alone within the gates to a courtyard: 閑, combining two pictographic elements more clearly visible in their early forms as 門 (gate) and 木 (tree). Or in its alternate form, a moon shining through open gates: 閒, which replaces 木 with 月 (moon).

Those artist-intellectuals often drank wine as an aid in cultivating this *wu-wei* idleness: the great T'ang Dynasty poet Po Chü-i (a very serious Ch'an practitioner) was uttering a witty cultural truism when he famously said that wine was as good as Ch'an for awakening. Indeed, drinking wine in Chinese poetry was generally used as a concise way of indicating a state of enlightenment. Artist-intellectuals recognized the effortless and spontaneous movement of Way as an ontological kind of idleness; and so, they took idleness as a spiritual ideal, living their everyday lives as a kind of meditative wander in which they moved with that effortless spontaneity of Way. Wang Wei even equates idleness with no-mind in this line: "no mind the whole day through, I keep idleness always whole."

Wu-wei is also a fundamental assumption guiding artistic practice, appearing perhaps most dramatically in calligraphy like the scroll reproduced on page 102. This is calligraphy in its wildest most artistic mode. Virtually all great calligraphers were serious Ch'an students who generally considered meditation and often wine to be essential preparation for creating such calligraphy. For them, this wild calligraphy was conceived as a form of Ch'an practice or teaching: wild empty-mind moving with the selfless spontaneity of Tao or *tzu-jan*. It was a way of moving there in that generative moment where the Cosmos perennially creates itself, for when a calligrapher first touches inked brush to a blank sheet of silk, it is that originary moment where Presence emerges from Absence. And as the brush-stroke traces through its arcs and twists, it is always there at that originary moment, just like awakened mind. It is *wu-wei* become visible: an awakened mind moving with the unbridled energy of the Cosmos itself, Presence tumbling through its myriad transformations.

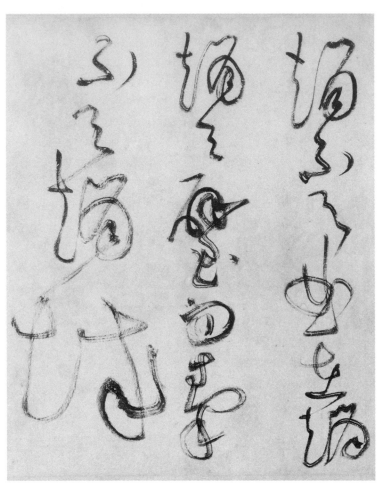

Huang T'ing-chien (1045–1105): *Biographies of Lien P'o and Lin Hsiang-jun* (1095). Detail.
Metropolitan Museum of Art, New York

禅

Meditation

MEDITATION AS AN INTENSE AND FORMAL-ized cultivation of empty-mind stillness—that was *dhyana*'s primary contribution to Taoism, the main catalyst that transformed Taoism into Ch'an. Etymologically, *dhyana* means something like "to fix the mind upon"—hence, meditation as controlling the mind, fixing the mind upon emptiness and tranquility. This kind of meditation is mentioned in the seminal Taoist texts, as in Lao Tzu's poetic descriptions: "polish the dark-enigma mirror / to a clarity beyond stain" and "inhabit the furthest peripheries of emptiness / and abide in the tranquil center." But the ancient Taoists never developed meditation into a formalized technique, so far as we know. It was much more individualistic, and it was always part of a larger practice. And in the end, after absorbing *dhyana* practice, Ch'an similarly moved beyond *dhyana* and returned meditation to the larger practice native to its Taoist origins.

The nirvana-tranquility of *dhyana*'s empty-mind meditation might be seen as a stage in both personal practice and the historical development of Ch'an. Bodhidharma, for example, at the "official" beginning of Ch'an, said that through *dhyana* we can "see original-nature." But *dhyana* was only a way to begin. Prajna-Able, the Sixth Patriarch, advised:

> Don't listen to me talk about emptiness, and then just devote yourself to emptiness. This is the most important of all things: don't devote yourself to emptiness. If you just empty the mind and sit in serene tranquility, you're devoting yourself to a blank and traceless emptiness.

And almost two centuries later, Purport Dark-Enigma described people practicing this form of meditation—"arresting the flow of thought, they don't let it rise; they hate noise and seek stillness"—and then he denounced it because it violates the free movement of Tao.

Mature Ch'an goes beyond empty-mind stillness to inhabit original-nature as Tao or *tzu-jan*. Lao Tzu described meditation as "sitting still in Way's company." And Prajna-Able said "Mind all clarity absolute is the fieldland of Tao." This seems almost the exact opposite of *dhyana*, for it cultivates mind moving according to its nature, spontaneously and unrestrained, rather than clutching at stillness and emptiness.

Indeed, for Sixth Patriarch Prajna-Able, meditation was about "seeing original-nature," rather than cultivating *dhyana* tranquility in the search for some kind of liberation:

> My wise and understanding friends, in this dharma-gate, sitting *ch'an* at origins has nothing to do with mind and nothing to do with purity. And I never talk about stillness. People speak of gazing at mind, but mind is at origins illusion. And since illusions are mere mirage, what is there to see? People speak of gazing at purity, but our original-nature is original source-tissue purity—even

when illusory thoughts hide from us this existence-tissue
all clarity absolute.[30]

And Prajna-Able's influential dharma-heir, Spirit-Lightning
Gather, said that "no-thought is just sitting in samadhi-
meditation stillness. *Ch'an*, on the other hand, *Ch'an* is all
about seeing original-nature."

We have seen how Ch'an meditation reweaves consciousness and earth/Cosmos by emptying away the structures of
self, leaving empty-mind mirroring the ten thousand things,
thereby replacing self-identity with identity as *tzu-jan*, Tao's
great transformation of things. But *wu-wei* as a foundational
cultural assumption adds dramatic new dimensions to meditative practice—dimensions that initially seem contrary to
the cultivation of empty-mind, and that led Ch'an masters like
Prajna-Able to criticize meditation when practiced simply as
dhyana's cultivation of empty-mind tranquility.

As it is nothing other than Absence, generative source of
both thought and the ten thousand things, empty-mind is not
simply an empty space of stillness or tranquility. Hence, Ch'an
meditation reveals that seeming tranquility as something
much deeper: a vast dark-enigma darkness, the generative tissue that is nothing less than the tumultuous source constantly
burgeoning forth into the ongoing transformations of the Cosmos. This is mind as dharma-master, as Buddha, as always already awakened.

For Ch'an, meditation's cultivation of emptiness is only a
way of clearing away the machinery of self and returning to see
with clarity that source and its movements. Hence, the fundamental form of mature Ch'an meditation not as *dhyana* cultivation of tranquility, a polishing of the mind-mirror, but as

wu-wei practice: meditation not just as *tzu-jan* occurrence witnessed in empty mirror-mind awareness, but as *wu-wei* participation in the process of *tzu-jan*. And awakening as the recognition of that as "original-nature."

Rather than a struggle to empty all mental activity away, Ch'an recognizes thought as part of *tzu-jan* or Tao: exactly like streamwater, for instance, moving sometimes deep and still, sometimes swirling and headlong. And in a passage about meditation from the *Platform Sutra of the Sixth Patriarch*, Prajna-Able describes the cosmological dimensions of thinking as part of original-nature:

> Thought thinks the original source-tissue nature of this existence-tissue all clarity absolute. This existence-tissue all clarity absolute is the potency of thought, and thought is the expression of this existence-tissue. In it's own original-nature, this existence-tissue all clarity absolute rises into thought—and even tangled through perception like sight and hearing, it never stains the ten thousand mirrored things. So, you move always composed and free.[31]

Potency (體) and *expression* (用) (which we encountered briefly in the footnote on p. 65) are important cosmological/ontological concepts in Chinese philosophy. *Potency* refers to the inherent potentiality or nature of things that gives shape to their particular *expression*, or "instantiation/manifestation" in the world. This is, as always in Taoist/Ch'an thought, not a metaphysical dimension to things, but the nature inherent to a thing—and as such it is virtually synonymous with inner-pattern (p. 75) and *ch'i*-thought/mind (p. 39 f.). In simple contemporary terms, Prajna-Able is saying that thought is the Cosmos thinking itself. And so, thought is itself always already awakened: there is no need for a meditative struggle to quell it.

This approach came naturally to Ch'an because, as we have seen (p. 39 f.), thought is 意: hence, *ch'i*-thought woven wholly into the ever-generative *ch'i*-tissue, into a living and "intelligent" Cosmos. It may seem unlikely that our trivial and obsessive train of thought is the movement of the Cosmos/ Tao, the Cosmos thinking itself: deep philosophy perhaps, but the everyday trivia? And yet, isn't that typical of the Cosmos? It's mostly trivial and repetitive: same galaxies, stars, and planets over and over, same seasons and grasses and insects, same days and nights and . . . same thoughts and feelings.

Original-nature is *tzu-jan* occurrence in perpetual movement. And not only the movement of thought. Empty mirror-mind perception too participates in the movement of *tzu-jan*: the ten thousand things of this Cosmos becoming us one after another after another, going inside us and vanishing there—that too is part of the great transformation of things. Hence: as a matter of actual experience, perception also is *wu-wei* action.

And so, in yet another instance of Ch'an's insistence on dismantling itself, we find Ch'an razing the very practice that gives it its name: *dhyana*, empty-mind meditation. We find as well another version of the Ch'an insight that we are always already enlightened, that there is no awakening to be discovered in meditation because whatever happens in consciousness is already *wu-wei*, and therefore already enlightened. And that entails a profound acceptance of oneself, a potentially transformative aspect of Ch'an practice.

This represents the subjective experience of the essential identity of Absence and Presence. Presence burgeons forth from Absence and so is essentially part of Absence. Or

107

put another way, it is Absence seen in its differentiated form. Thought (Presence) is as much Tao as no-thought (Absence), and is therefore as enlightened, which is why Ch'an masters often ridiculed meditation practiced as the mere pursuit of emptiness and stillness. This is a bedrock insight that has a long history in China, stretching back to the beginnings of Taoist thought: in Lao Tzu, for instance, who spoke of "sitting still in Way's company." Or Wang Pi, the seminal philosopher in Dark-Enigma Learning, which was crucial in the creation of Ch'an through the amalgamation of Buddhist and Taoist thought/practice. In his commentary to the *I Ching*, the earliest of Taoist texts, Wang Pi begins a passage addressing Absence and Presence with:

> Return means turning back to the source-tissue, and that source-tissue is the very mind of all heaven and earth itself. Wherever activity ceases, stillness begins; but there's no opposition between movement and stillness. Wherever words end, silence begins; but there's no opposition between silence and words.

In speaking of "no opposition between movement and stillness," Wang Pi is describing the unity of Absence and Presence in the empirical Cosmos; and in speaking of "no opposition between silence and words," he is describing the unity of Absence and Presence in the realm of consciousness. Already, here in proto-Ch'an Chinese philosophy, we have a description of mature Ch'an practice. And it will be described again and again in various ways by the Ch'an masters to come. Purport Dark-Enigma, to take an example using the same terminology, said "Movement and stillness are both Absence's own original-nature . . . a person of Tao who depends on nothing makes use of both movement and stillness."

Returning to Ch'an's Taoist roots, *wu-wei* as the very form of consciousness appears already in Lao Tzu's *Tao Te Ching*, with its seminal description of *wu-wei* practice:

> a sage abides in the realm of Absence's own action [*wu-wei*]
> living out that wordless teaching.
> The ten thousand things arise without beginnings there,
> abide without waiting there,
> come to perfection without dwelling there.
>
> Without dwelling there: that's the one way
> you'll never lose it.

As is so often the case with Lao Tzu, there is no distinction here between subjective and objective realms. It sounds like he's talking about empirical reality, but it feels like he's talking about the realm of consciousness. Those ten thousand things could be occurrence appearing as objective facts, or as subjective facts such as thoughts and memories. So in its very form, this passage asserts a unity of subjective and objective as a single tissue of *tzu-jan* occurrence.

Without dwelling there: that is the crucial thing. It means accepting the movement of thought or life as part of Tao's great transformation, rather than clinging to a permanent self, a stable and enduring center of identity that sustains itself in turn by clinging to a constellation of assumptions and ideas. Yellow-Bitterroot Mountain describes this non-dwelling in terms of mental process, where Ch'an meditation might be described as thought not anchored to self as some entity outside change: "Right now, thought following thought after thought: just don't dwell in it." And we have seen Chuang Tzu describing it in terms of empty mirror-mind:

Live empty, perfectly empty.

Sage masters always employ mind like a pure mirror: welcome nothing, refuse nothing,

reflect everything, hold nothing.

Prajna-Able calls this non-dwelling the root of his "dharma-gate," his teaching. After criticizing meditation conceived as the simple pursuit of *dhyana* emptiness and tranquility, he says: "A mind not dwelling anywhere in dharma's world of things: it's Tao flowing through freely." And he further describes meditation as simply sitting

without motion and without stillness, without birth and without death, without leaving and without coming, without good and without bad, without dwelling and without setting out—all in the simplest stillness and quiet. That is the great Way [Tao].

And Ch'an's sage-master wrecking-crew dismantles the Ch'an practice of *wu-wei* too, insisting that *wu-wei* is simply the structure of anyone's everyday experience, that we are all therefore already enlightened. And simple empirical observation confirms this. If we search our actual moment-to-moment experience for that permanent self we assume directs our thoughts and actions, we find nothing. In the actual process of doing things, like washing dishes or planting a garden, we can find no self acting. It is only when we reflect on the action that we inject a self, and we do that only because of our cultural assumptions. The same is true of thinking or feeling. We assume these private mental activities to be the quintessential arena of self, but again: if we examine what is actually happening when we think, we can't find any trace of a self. It is, again, those cultural assumptions that make us say thinking is the activity of a self.

Ch'an's *wu-wei* meditation is simply a way of "seeing" that fact as our "original-nature." It is a way of seeing that, liberated from the self anchoring us outside/against *tzu-jan*'s vast movement, we are always already "wandering boundless and free through the selfless unfolding of things" (as Chuang Tzu describes it on pp. 118–19). Or indeed, *as* the boundless transformation of things. And self, when it does arise, is only part of that drift, is therefore a kind of "selfless self." Chuang Tzu speaks of this mind wandering several times:

> Let your mind wander the pure and simple. . . . Blend your *ch'i* into the boundless, follow occurrence [*tzu-jan*] appearing in things of itself and don't let selfhood get in the way.[32]

> Just let your mind wander along in the drift of things. Trust yourself to what is beyond you—let it be the nurturing center. Then you've made it. In the midst of all this, is there really any response? Nothing can compare to simply living out your inevitable nature. And there's nothing more difficult.

Ch'an meditation is not an attempt to suppress thought processes, but simply a way to reduce things stimulating thought, thereby allowing us to "see original-nature." It reveals stillness too as part of *tzu-jan* occurrence. And further, it allows us to inhabit that stillness at the source of *wu-wei* movement, which is a remarkable and emotionally powerful (心 as "heart" in addition to "mind") kind of intimacy with the very origin of the Cosmos. In this intimacy, awakening is not empty-mind tranquility. It is instead to move freely and selflessly with change, living a simultaneity in which inner and outer move as a single tissue of thought and perception woven through empirical fact and event. And it is a simultaneity in perpetual motion and transformation that continues only imperceptibly changed after death. Hence, awakening as Chunag Tzu's *wu-wei* practice of "wandering boundless and free through the selfless unfolding of things."

公案

Sangha-Case

MEDITATION IS THE HEART OF CH'AN PRAC-tice, its primary means of understanding the nature of consciousness and coming to inhabit that generative origin-moment/place. Ch'an's form of meditation is at bottom a form of *wu-wei* practice, and it is supplemented by another quite different form of *wu-wei* practice: sangha-case training. Ch'an literature (written and oral) existed primarily as "records" of the lives and teachings of Ch'an masters. These records contained many moments of poetic distillation: enigmatic sayings and wild antics intended to upend reason and dismantle conceptual structures. These moments of story and fable operated with poetic immediacy, rather than the usual discursive or explanatory use of language. They were performative, enacting insight rather than explaining it. Eventually, Ch'an teachers began drawing especially revealing moments from these records, moments that distill the essential insights of Ch'an, and assigning them as puzzles for students to ponder, as for example the perplexing answers to the question "What is Buddha" (p. 86), or those from the *Blue-Cliff Record* suggesting thusness is the essence of Ch'an

113

(pp. 64–65), or these especially concise fables also from the *Blue-Cliff Record*:

A monk asked Hundred-Elder Mountain: "What is the grand and wondrous affair?"

"To sit alone on Valiant-Vast Mountain," replied Hundred-Elder.

The monk bowed. Hundred-Elder struck him a blow. [chapter 26]

Head-monk Samadhi-Still asked Purport Dark-Enigma: "What is the Buddha-dharma's great *ch'i*-mind meaning?"

Dark-Enigma descended from his meditation seat, grabbed hold of Samadhi-Still and gave him a single slap, then pushed him away.

Samadhi-Still froze and just stood there.

"Head-monk Samadhi-Still," called out another monk, "why don't you bow?"

Samadhi-Still thereupon bowed reverently, and suddenly had a great awakening. [chapter 32]

A monk asked Cloud-Gate Mountain: "What is the entrance every fleck of dust offers into samadhi's three-shadowed earth?"

Cloud-Gate replied: "Rice in the rice-bowl, water in the water-pail." [chapter 50]

Such scraps of story came to be known as *kung-an* (公案, now widely known in its Japanese pronunciation: *koan*), and they were gathered into collections for use by later teachers and students. Thus was created a remarkable new form of Chinese literature, the best-known examples of which being the *Blue-Cliff Record* (1125) and *No-Gate Gateway* (1228)—

114

though that sense of the wild and paradoxical suffuses the seminal Taoist texts: *Tao Te Ching* and *Chuang Tzu*. And in the latter, Ch'an-like stories and fables proliferate, often functioning very much like sangha-cases:

When Lao Tzu died, Modest-Ease went in to mourn for him. He shouted three times, then left.

Kung-an means a "court case," and more literally a "public case." The term was adapted to the Ch'an situation for a number of reasons. Ch'an masters originally conducted *kung-an* training in "public," when the monastic community was gathered together. A *kung-an* is a factual situation that needs to be "understood" accurately, like a court case. And finally, each *kung-an* represents a kind of precedent to which later practitioners can refer. Hence: "sangha-case," *sangha* meaning "a Buddhist community."

Like meditation, sangha-cases are a means of resolving what is the most fundamental question for Ch'an practice, and perhaps for human consciousness in general: how to move past the illusory separation between consciousness and Cosmos, which entails erasing the seeming separation between thought and silence, subjective and objective, mind and landscape, self and Cosmos. To do this, sangha-case practice used paradox to instill doubt and confusion, to deconstruct logical thought and explanation, eventually dismantling the very structures of self, whereupon the student acts without thought, spontaneously and selflessly. As in meditation, this returns consciousness to its original empty-mind nature: empty-mind that precludes the distancing of things as objects, allowing an immediate experience of landscape's ten thousand things in and of themselves, as elemental mystery. Sangha-case practice also reveals empty-mind as indistinguishable from the elemental mystery of Tao's great transformation—and as that great transformation is boundless and inexhaustible, consciousness is revealed as boundless and inexhaustible.

With its paradox and wild antics, sangha-case training may seem daunting; but once we understand how it works, it becomes quite straightforward. Like Ch'an meditation, sangha-case practice is most fundamentally *wu-wei* practice. And indeed, the two were closely related in the monastery, for it was meditation's cultivation of empty-mind that prepared one to act from the generative Absence of empty-mind in response to a sangha-case. From the beginning, when Ch'an teachers examined students, they looked for a student who moved in a direct and single-minded way—forceful, without self-doubt or hesitation—for that was a student who had mastered *wu-wei*. And when that examination process was formalized into sangha-case training, *wu-wei* was the guiding assumption.

Solutions to sangha-cases always involve responding inside the enigma and with a spontaneous immediacy operating at a level that precedes thought and analysis. The correct answer to a sangha-case is never a seemingly reasoned and appropriate response. Instead, it is whatever emerges spontaneously from that silent emptiness where the logical construction of thoughts has not yet begun, and such answers are only possible when a student has come to inhabit the wholeness of *wu*-mind ("no-mind/Absence-mind") at that generative origin-moment/place, a habitation that is cultivated in meditation practice. Hence, at the cosmological/ontological level, the response is *wu*-mind ("Absence-mind") moving at the most profound level as *wu-wei* ("Absence-action").

Such responses take two forms: spoken words or physical action. When a sangha-case plays out in words, it grows directly

116

out of a meditative understanding of *wu-wei* in consciousness: an understanding in which thoughts are not the calculating machinery of an isolated self, but instead emerge with selfless spontaneity from that origin-moment/place. Hence, thought as Tao or *tzu-jan* occurrence. Ch'an masters described this mental process as already awakened, in contrast to the convenional *dhyana* idea of enlightenment as the perfection of thoughtless and tranquil emptiness.

And as physical action, a "correct" response is not unlike a master calligrapher at work (p. 100 f.): selfless action as integral to the unfurling Cosmos, action moving with the dynamic energy of the Cosmos. But it is also meant to replace words and ideas with the sheer thusness of things, the master's wild and surprising antics startling the student's mind out of analytical thought and into the immediate empty-mind experience of that thusness.

Either way, words or actions, sangha-cases are about *enacting* awakening, rather than explaining it. They cultivate that sage belonging as an organic part of the great transformation of things. Here again is why Ch'an is described as a teaching outside of words and ideas. Even when words are used, they are used not for what they say, but for what they *enact*. In this, like meditation, sangha-case training directly transmits that experience of empty-mind belonging.

We find the roots of this practice in Kuo Hsiang, one of the great Dark-Enigma Learning philosophers who offered this distillation:

The ten thousand things can only take *tzu-jan* as their source. It is *wu-wei* action that makes *tzu-jan tzu-jan*....
If you move as *wu-wei*, you're self-reliant; and so, act as source.

117

This self-reliance of *wu-wei* action as the source is crucial to Ch'an: in meditation, but perhaps most apparently, in sangha-case practice. It is in this self-reliance that one succeeds in sangha-case training, self-reliance that is radically transformative and liberating; and it was described that way from the beginning, as in this passage from Lao Tzu that might describe meditation, though in its play on the double meaning of 無 ("not/Absence"), it is perhaps an even better description of sangha-case training:

To work at learning brings more each day.
To work at Way brings less each day,
less and still less
until you're Absence's own doing/action [*wu-wei*].
And when you're Absence's own doing/action, there's
    nothing [*wu*] you don't do/act [*wei*].

In *wu-wei*, we live integral to Tao, the Cosmos as the generative tissue that "does" everything. So, just as there is nothing Tao/Cosmos doesn't do, "there's nothing you don't do." And again, as that great transformation is boundless and inexhaustible, we are boundless and inexhaustible, and therefore radically "self-reliant." This represents liberation not only from the conscribed limitation and alienation of self, but also from death, for death can only apply to that now-vanished identity-center self. This is self-reliance as radical liberation. In an account remarkably similar to descriptions we will see of awakening in the Ch'an literature, Chuang Tzu described those who have mastered that liberation as moving with a radical self-reliance in which they live a cosmological kind of wild freedom:

Companions in their realm to the Maker-of-Things [Tao],
they're in human form for now, wandering the one *ch'i*

that breathes through all heaven and earth. For them, life is a useless appendage, a swollen tumor, and death is like a boil breaking open or pus draining from a festering sore. So how would they choose between life and death, before and after?

On loan from everything else, they'll soon be entrusted back to the one body. Forgetting liver and gallbladder, abandoning ears and eyes, they'll continue on again, tumbling and twirling through a blur of endings and beginnings. They roam at ease beyond the tawdry dust of this world, Absence's own doing/action [*wu-wei*] wandering boundless and free through the selfless unfolding of things.[33]

無生

Unborn

IT WOULD MAKE SENSE TO SAY DEATH TOO IS Buddha, for death is also a great teacher. Although the emergence and vanishing of *tzu-jan*'s generative process is all around us—woodpeckers tapping on hollowed out trees and tin mailboxes, thoughts appearing and vanishing, gusting wind and changing seasons—it isn't easy to experience oneself as integral to that process. That is, at bottom, a large part of what Ch'an practice is about: *wu-wei* practice in meditation, in sangha-case training, or simply in day-to-day life. But facing the prospect of death without illusions, as ancient Chinese artist-intellectuals did, our belonging to *tzu-jan* occurrence becomes an overwhelmingly real and unavoidable fact. For in death we vanish absolutely back into *tzu-jan*'s process of appearance and disappearance. And so, death reveals yet again the Ch'an insight that practice is unnecessary because we are always already enlightened.

In the Taoist/Ch'an framework, death is a return home, a return to the generative tissue, to (as Lao Tzu says) the "nurturing mother," the "mother of all beneath heaven." And there was solace in that. But seen at a deeper level, we never leave home. Absence and Presence are a single existence-tissue: the ten thousand things are not born out of Absence, never separate from Absence. And it's the same for us. It might seem that we are born out of Absence, that in death we return to Absence, which would be homecoming enough. And it makes sense to speak of it that way, as Purport Dark-Enigma does when he tells his disciples that they will "return to perennial Absence."[34] But however separate the center of identity may seem, with its thought and emotion and memory, it too is part of existence-tissue Absence, wholly *unborn*, as Patriarch Sudden-Horse Way-Entire said in a poem:

The inner-pattern and this world it shapes: they move unhindered, and so it is that everything born is unborn.

Our "unborn" lives are simply ripples in the movement of *ch'i*-tissue. And so, death was seen not as a grand personal tragedy, but as a natural transition in that movement. Death is only a problem when seen from the self-involved perspective of a personal identity that is "born." But as we have seen, Ch'an reveals the existence-tissue itself as our truest self; so there is no death, only a continuation of the great transformation.

Unborn is sometimes 不生, meaning simply "not born." But it is often 無生, as when Sixth Patriarch Prajna-Able speaks of "awakening to the sudden dharma of non-birth." 生 can mean either "born" or "living." And as in 無為 (*wu-wei*: no/Absence-action), 無 here plays once again on its double meaning: "not" and "Absence." Hence, 無生 becomes: "not/Absence + born/alive." From this comes "Absence-born" or "Absence-alive," describing our most essential identity as Absence itself. This suggests the cosmological/ontological depths of the simpler reading, "non-birth" or "unborn," and gives a second reading to Prajna-Able's statement: "awakening to the sudden dharma of Absence-born/alive."

At these depths, we are each a fleeting form conjured in Absence's generative process of perpetual transformation: not just born out of it and returned to it in death, which still assumes a center of identity detached from the Cosmos and its processes, but never out of it, totally unborn. Indeed, our fullest identity, being unborn, is Absence itself, is therefore deathless because it is all and none of earth's fleeting forms simultaneously. From this comes Yellow-Bitterroot Mountain's recognition that

> if your mind is unborn and thoughts arise—it's *tzu-jan*, not illusion. That's why they say "When mind is born, all sorts of dharmas are born. When mind is extinguished, all sorts of dharmas are extinguished."[35]

And elsewhere, Yellow-Bitterroot Mountain extends this to the heart of Ch'an wisdom: "when mind is unborn, *tzu-jan* itself becomes the great wisdom."[36]

The double meaning of 無 deepens Sangha-Fundament's already remarkably condensed declaration that we've read as "a sage's mastery of emptiness perfectly Absence-born/alive: that is the perspective of *prajna*-wisdom's dark-enigma mirror" (p. 92), for we can now read it as "a sage's mastery of emptiness perfectly unborn: that is the perspective of *prajna*-wisdom's dark-enigma mirror." And with its double reading, Sangha-Fundaments's declaration explicates Yellow-Bitterroot Mountain's teaching that "to penetrate the depths of Ch'an's Way, you must inhabit the full expanse of unborn mind."

This concept of non-birth infuses every aspect of Taoist/ Ch'an thought. We know our unborn nature directly in meditation, for in empty-mind one belongs without any separation to the Absence-tissue. Empty mirror-mind perception reveals our unborn nature through that identity of inner and outer in which empty awareness and the expansive presence of existence are whole. And whatever form it takes—meditation, sangha-case training, day-to-day life—*wu-wei* as practice returns us to our "unborn" nature, for in it we move as integral to generative Absence.

Yellow-Bitterroot Mountain considered non-birth the essence of Ch'an: "To penetrate the depths of Ch'an's Way, you must inhabit the full expanse of unborn mind."[37] Non-birth is a profound way of understanding the claim that we are always already enlightened. As we have seen, Prajna-Able says directly that understanding non-birth wholly is tantamount to awakening when he speaks of "awakening to the sudden dharma of non-birth." And finally, true to the Ch'an spirit of dismantling itself, Sudden-Horse Way-Entire declared that once we master non-birth we have no need for Ch'an:

> Once you understand mind to its furthest boundaries with perfect clarity, even frenetic tangles of thought are unborn [不生]. Once frenetic tangles of thought are unborn [不生], you've mastered the patient dharma of non-birth [無生: hence also "the patient dharma of Absence-born/alive"]. It was like this at the beginning and it's like this now, so why cultivate the Way or sit in *Ch'an* meditation? Not cultivating and not sitting: that is the clear and pure Ch'an of a Buddha in existence-tissue arrival.[38]

This provides another approach to the integration of self-identity and Tao/Cosmos. If we are unborn, whatever meaning we create is also unborn. Meaning is the Cosmos orienting itself. It is not a separate transcendental realm, a stable outside measure of existence. It is the Cosmos's way of knowing itself; and so, is no different than any other meaningless twist in the vast movement of the Cosmos: the twist of galaxies, the tectonic upthrust of mountain ranges, seasons, egrets hunting river shallows all patience. Meaning is meaningless, a principle informing the concept of *ch'i*-thought/ mind—the "intentionality/desire/intelligence" that shapes the ongoing cosmological process of change and transformation, and of which human intelligence is one particular manifestation. The Cosmos shapes itself into mountain and river, egrets startling up into flight and pear blossoms tumbling in the evening wind, and they explain nothing, mean nothing. It shapes itself into linguistic meaning the same way, and meaning explains nothing.

It makes sense that the definition of *Ch'an* is meditation, for meditation reveals virtually all of Ch'an's insights. And we find that true here again, for the meaninglessness of meaning is manifest in the way thoughts emerging from a generative emptiness are seen as the same *tzu-jan* process as the ten thousand things emerging in the empirical world. An idea emerges the way a mountain range emerges. Again, ordinary mind no different than the grand cosmological Tao, as we have seen Patriarch Sudden-Horse Way-Entire say with complete concision: "Ordinary mind is the Way." And as we have also seen, Ch'an meditation aspires finally not to some pure nirvana-tranquility, for it embraces the movement of thought as *tzu-jan* occurrence, as meaning that is meaningless. In the end, meaningless meaning reveals another dimension to Ch'an's skepticism about the explanatory power of words and ideas. Isn't meaninglessness what meditation and sangha-case practice finally reveal? This whole system of

Ch'an understanding also explains nothing, means nothing, returning us in the end to dark-enigma. Or what it explains, in its dark-enigma meaninglessness, is that our original-nature is unborn. And of course, to "see original-nature" is to be awakened.

見·性

Awakening

CH'AN OPERATES ON THE EDGE OF OUR HUMAN universe, where the human mingles away into the broader Cosmos. It takes a wild and fearless mind to inhabit that terrain, but only there is it possible to engage Ch'an at the deep levels necessary to awakening. For the adventure of Ch'an means dismantling all of the explanations and assumptions that structure our human universe, all of the answers that orient us and define us as centers of human identity. And because we can only be either inside or outside that cocoon of conceptual structures that define and orient us, awakening can only be, famously for Ch'an, instantaneous and complete.

In their deconstruction of conceptual structures through meditation and sangha-case training, Ch'an's wrecking-crew masters raze most essentially self, the center of identity that seems self-enclosed and outside natural process. What remains is mind itself, consciousness emptied of all content, which is itself awakening in the Bodhidharma poem we saw in the Introduction:

A separate transmission outside all teaching
and not founded in fine words of scripture,

126

it's simple: pointing directly at mind. There,
seeing original-nature, you become Buddha.

Here the Ch'an term for "awakening"—見性 (*chien-hsing*;
Jap. *kensho*), "seeing original-nature"—appears in the last line:

見	性	成	佛
see	original-nature	become	Buddha

The full expanse of this awakening appears in the line's grammar, the level of language that shapes consciousness most fundamentally. Following the rule for Chinese poems, there is no
grammatical subject/self who "sees." Instead, it is an absent
presence, an empty-mind that belongs to the Cosmos rather
than to a particular identity-center. The line's "original-nature"
also belongs to no one or thing in particular. And the same is
true of "become Buddha," where there is again no grammatical subject, only that empty-mind. As we have seen, *Buddha*
means most essentially that very empty-mind, so we have:
"Buddha becomes Buddha." Or remembering how Buddha
is synonymous with Tao/Way at Ch'an's deep cosmological/
ontological levels, the proposition is "Buddha-Way becomes
Buddha-Way." Prajna-Able makes this connection directly in
his version of this line: "seeing original-nature, [   ] becomes
Buddha-Way." And so, we have here in the grammar, another
form of the Ch'an's principle that we are always already awakened, always already Buddha.

It is similar in the other term for Ch'an awakening: 悟 (*wu*;
Jap. *satori*), composed etymologically of *mind* (心 appearing
here in stylized form as 忄 on the left) and *me* (吾) on the right.
This renders the term's common meaning of "waking" (from
sleep) as a suddenly renewed awareness of "my mind." And

that becomes in the Ch'an context something very close to a "sudden awakening" (that essential Ch'an principle) to empty-mind as "original-nature." Indeed, Prajna-Able speaks of the "mind-ground" (心地) as the source of awakening (悟), which he describes as an "awakening to your own original nature" involving no "precepts, meditation, or wisdom."

Under either name, Ch'an awakening transforms immediate day-to-day experience. It replaces the identity-center's alienation from existence with a mirror-deep intimacy, a "sincerity" in which outside becomes inside and inside outside. But that is only the beginning. In Ch'an awakening, thoughts and by extension all actions move as *wu-wei*, which means they move integral to *tzu-jan*'s movement. The grand assumption defining Ch'an's two primary forms of practice, meditation and sangha-case training, this *wu-wei* also defines the goal of those practices: awakening, in the distinctively Ch'an sense. Hence, Ch'an practice returns from *dhyana* Buddhism to its Taoist roots, as in this description of sagehood and awakening by Yellow-Bitterroot Mountain: "When body and mind move as *tzu-jan*, you fathom Tao and understand mind." And just after that, in a passage we have already seen, he continues:

> The ancients had sharp minds all wild bounty. Hearing even a single word, they gave up all learning. And so they were called those who gave up learning and mastered the *wu-wei* idleness of Tao.

In this awakening redefined by Taoism, we live in a selfless simultaneity of inner and outer moving together at that generative origin-moment/place, inner and outer woven into a single tissue of thought, perception, and empirical fact: movement dynamic and all transformation through and through, sometimes still and sometimes moving, sometimes tranquil and sometimes tempestuous, sometimes thinking and sometimes silent/empty. In this awakening, we inhabit life wholly and immediately, belonging utterly and moving at origins.

The Ch'an wrecking-crew insists over and over that we are already awakened, that there is nothing to practice—because the mirror is always wide-open and flawless, and because mind can only move as *wu-wei*. So in awakening, the Ch'an adventure returns to its beginnings in immediate everyday experience. But now, that everyday experience is transformed into 禪 (*Ch'an*): "the Cosmos alone simply and exhaustively with itself." And with that transformation, everyday experience is simply the Cosmos seeing itself, the Cosmos thinking itself, the Cosmos feeling itself.

Remembering that 心 is not just "mind," but also "heart," we can begin to feel the emotional dimensions of awakening. For with that profound sense of belonging as integral to the vast living Cosmos comes an exhilarating sea-swell of heart-mind emotion—joy and tranquility, beauty and ecstasy, boundlessness, wonder, awe, and grief, because the great transformation necessarily includes attrition and loss—all suffusing the sense of radical wildness and freedom that comes of existing not as a circumscribed identity-center, but as integral to a dynamic and generative Cosmos, a radical wildness and freedom become the nature of immediate everyday experience.

In this belonging to Tao's cosmological process of creation and destruction, we return to Sixth Patriarch Prajna-Able's "awakening to the sudden dharma of non-birth." And we have seen Spirit-Lightning Gather, dharma-heir to the Sixth Patriarch, say that the essence of awakened *prajna*-wisdom is simply "seeing Absence" (見無), his variation on the standard term for awakening: "seeing original-nature" (見性).

129

Hence, to "see original-nature" is to "see Absence," which is to see yourself as unborn ("Absence born/alive"), and therefore inseparable from the cosmological/ontological process of Absence unfurling through its vast transformations.

This liberation hinges on completely giving up the anchor of a permanent self seemingly outside of Tao's vast movement, as in Patriarch Sudden-Horse Way-Entire's answer when asked about the essence of Buddha-dharma: "It's simply where you are when you let go of that self you happen to be." There, one exists not as an identity-center, but as unborn, as the whole of Tao's great transformation moving perennially at that generative origin-moment/place. For without the anchor of self, we are returned to our "original-nature" indistinguishable from the vast and enduring Cosmos itself. Then we move through everyday experience with the tranquility of the Cosmos: we "wander boundless and free through the selfless unfolding of things," free even of death itself—for when death comes, it comes as Tao's great transformation of things simply unfurling its next possibility. And because that great transformation of things is inexhaustible, we are now inexhaustible. Inexhaustible in the radical freedom of a cosmological/ontological kind of liberation, as Sudden-Horse Way-Entire suggests in a further description of his "Buddha-dharma":

> The dharma of all things themselves, that is the Buddha-dharma. All those dharmas together are liberation, and that liberation is the existence-tissue all clarity absolute.

Chuang Tzu puts it like this: "Make the inexhaustible your body / and wander beyond origins," which recalls his description of liberation as a wild cosmological freedom (pp. 118–19), or this very similar description:

If you mount the source of heaven and earth and the ten thousand changes, if you ride the six seasons of *ch'i* in their endless dispute—then you travel the inexhaustible, depending on nothing at all. Hence the saying: *The realized remain selfless. The sacred remain meritless. The enlightened remain nameless.*

He describes a sage living day-to-day life similarly:

For such a person, [birth and death] change nothing. All heaven and earth could be churned over and falling apart, but for him nothing would be lost. He inquires where nothing is false, and he isn't tossed about as things shift back and forth. He knows the endless transformation of things follows its own inevitable nature, and he holds fast to the ancestral source.

And as we've seen above, the proto-Ch'an Dark-Enigma Learning philosopher Kuo Hsiang describes liberation similarly half a millennium later in his commentary on Chuang Tzu:

no-mind inhabits the mystery of things. . . . This is the importance of being at the hinge of Tao, for there you can know dark-enigma's extent. There your movements range free.

The liberation of unborn and non-dwelling awakening is no different in the Ch'an literature. Sixth Patriarch Prajna-Able says:

Once you see original-nature—you dwell in neither inner nor outer, and so of yourself come and go freely. You cast aside the mind that clings to this or that, and so move unhindered through the unfurling of things.

131

Here we find fully developed the implications of the non-dwelling that Prajna-Able described as the root of his "dharma-gate," his teaching (p. 110). In essence, this non-dwelling means the center of identity shifted from self to Tao; and because Tao is all appearance and disappearance in a process of perennial transformation, non-dwelling is a liberation in which we dwell nowhere, cling to nothing, depend on nothing. With that, we move as the "boundless and free" Cosmos itself.

Wang Wei, the quintessential Ch'an rivers-and-mountains poet, describes in his memorial inscription for the Sixth Patriarch how Prajna-Able taught that Ch'an insight means to be "unborn and therefore without an *I*," and that "*prajna*-wisdom is to depend on nothing." As we saw before, Wang describes *wu-wei* as the essence of awakening for Prajna-Able, and *wu-wei* is virtually synonymous with non-dwelling. Wang further describes Prajna-Able as a master of *wu-wei* who has seen through the distinction between Absence and Presence. And in the poetic preface to the memorial inscription's more prosaic account of Prajna-Able's life, Wang describes the actual experience of this Absence-action awakening in terms by now familiar:

Done giving up Presence, we
penetrate the source of Presence.
Done dwelling in emptiness, we
fathom the origin of emptiness.
When movement is all stillness
we ride transformation perennial,
inhabiting the hundred dharmas endlessly,
suffusing the ten thousand things boundlessly.

Tu Fu, the greatest of Chinese poets and a friend of Wang Wei's, invests this idea of non-dwelling with the dimensions of landscape practice when he describes himself at a Ch'an monastery turning to look out across mountains and saying it was to "look into mind that dwells nowhere." Radical non-dwelling appears again when Purport Dark-Enigma describes our ordinary moment-to-moment mind as already an awakening in which we move "freely" through "life and death and coming and going," because we have "no form, no characteristics, no root, no source, and no dwelling-place" (the *no* here is 無, which in its meaning as "Absence" gives: "form Absence and characteristics Absence, root Absence and source Absence, and dwelling-place too Absence"). And as we have seen, he further proposes that once awakened to our inherent Buddha-nature, we "ride the surge of circumstances," "a person of Tao dependent upon nothing," and he calls this the "dark-enigma of all Buddhas." Not surprisingly for the Ch'an wrecking-crew, Sudden-Horse Way-Entire pushed the principle of non-dwelling to its limit, dismantling even *wu-wei* when he said that awakening means "never dwelling in *wu-wei*."

The dimensions of this non-dwelling become clear when Sudden-Horse Way-Entire describes the liberation of awakening to inherent Buddha-nature through many of the cosmological/ontological concepts that we have seen (Buddha, Absence, Presence, dharma, inner-pattern, unborn, non-dwelling, existence-tissue, emptiness) and one that we have not—loom of origins, a mythological version of an origin-place that weaves out the fabric of reality:

A Buddha is capable of open-heartedness, but possesses *prajna*-wisdom and is well-versed in the loom of origins, its inner workings. Once a Buddha, you break through the net of doubt everything alive shares, leave the tangles of Absence and Presence far behind. And you're done with all feelings, a sage-master knowing people and dharma

133

are both empty. Turning with the wheel of Absence, you stride beyond all measurement or limit, and everything you do is unhindered, so you penetrate through both inner-pattern and this world it shapes.

Then you're like a cloud appearing in the sky, suddenly, and then suddenly disappearing without a trace.* Or like writing on water.

Unborn and undying, you know nirvana's great stillness and extinction. When you're caught in life's tangles, it's the storehouse giving birth to all existence-tissue arrival. Free of life's tangles, it's the great body of dharma. As the dharma body, you are boundless and essentially without increase or decrease. You can be large or small, square or round. Corresponding to the forms things take, like a moon in water, you ride the steady flood of it all: never standing still and never planting roots, never exhausting Presence-action and never dwelling even in Absence-action [*wu-wei*]. Presence-action is the home Absence-action uses; and Absence-action is the home Presence-action depends on. But once a Buddha, you don't dwell even in that dependence. And so they say you are "existence-tissue perfectly empty and depending on nothing."†

Dismantling the Buddhist idea of nirvana as some kind of transcendental tranquility-bliss, Sudden-Horse here redefines *nirvana* as the "stillness" of the Cosmos steadily unfurling its

---

* There's a more philosophical reading rustling below the surface here: "suddenly Presence and then vanishing into Absence again without a trace."

† Or: "like pure emptiness depending on nothing."

vast transformations. And so, it is a tranquility that comes with awakening in which we "wander boundless and free through the selfless unfolding of things." This is the tranquility Ch'an offers: not the simple *dhyana*-tranquility of a mind emptied through *dhyana* meditation, but the tranquility of moving integral to this Cosmos slowly opening through its possibilities.

As we have seen, Hsieh Ling-yün described enlightenment as dwelling integral to the inner-pattern that shapes this unfurling, a state that is realized through meditative practice:

Become Absence and mirror the whole, then you're returned to the final and total enlightenment of inner-pattern understood clear through to the end.

A contemporary of Hsieh's, in a letter to the proto-Ch'an Buddhist Sangha-Fundament, used the same terms:

A sage's mind is dark and still. And in the enlightenment of inner-pattern understood clear through to the end, it's no different than Absence.

Bodhidharma described "awakening all clarity absolute" as "abiding in the inner-pattern" where "a serene mind is all *wu-wei*." Sixth Patriarch Prajna-Able, as we have seen, said that when we "see original-nature" we're "awakened to the vastness of *ch'i*-mind," *ch'i-mind* being a virtual synonym for *inner-pattern*. And Yellow-Bitterroot Mountain called awakening "the *wu-wei* idleness of Tao."

In the *dhyana* Buddhism that migrated to China from India, *samadhi* simply meant "consciousness emptied of all subjective content." But it was transliterated into Chinese as 三昧地, which means "three-shadowed earth." That begins to suggest *samadhi*'s meaning in Ch'an: empty-mind free of all conceptual structures, self dismantled completely by the Ch'an wrecking-crew, leaving consciousness open to its "original-nature" as the Cosmos moving in perfect tranquility at that all-encompassing and perennial origin-place that Lao Tzu called *Absence. No-Gate Gateway,* the great sangha-case collection, says that in this samadhi-awakening we "wander all heaven and earth in a single stride." It says awakening comes after devoting all our energy to understanding origin-tissue Absence, Absence that *No-Gate Gateway* calls the "gateway of our ancestral patriarchs." And *No-Gate Gateway* goes on to describe this awakening in grand and visionary terms reminiscent of Chuang Tzu, terms that recall the etymological meaning of the Ch'an ideogram, its pictographic elements suggesting "the Cosmos alone simply and exhaustively with itself":

> Let all the delusions of a lifetime go, all the understanding and insight; and slowly, little by little, nurture the simplicity of occurrence appearing of itself [*tzu-jan*].[39]
>
> Soon, inner and outer are a single tissue. A single tissue, and you're like a mute in the midst of dream: all that understanding for yourself alone. Then suddenly, the whole thing breaks wide-open, and all heaven and earth shudder in astonishment.... If you meet Buddha, you kill Buddha. If you meet ancestral patriarchs, you kill ancestral patriarchs.
>
> Out there walking the cliff-edge between life and death, you're perfectly self-possessed, vast and wide-open in such wild freedom. Through all four transformations in the six forms of existence, you wander the playfulness of samadhi's three-shadowed earth.

And all the while, it's just everyday ordinary mind!

APPENDIX:
LOST IN TRANSLATION

CH'AN'S CONCEPTUAL FRAMEWORK IS ALMOST ENTIRELY absent in the literature of Zen in English—whether in books about Zen, books by Zen roshis presenting their teachings, or translations of the original Ch'an literature from ancient China (many done by Zen teachers). From this it follows that the conceptual world of original Ch'an must be also absent in contemporary Zen teaching and practice, that direct transmission outside of texts. The absence of original Ch'an in books about Zen cannot be shown beyond the simple statement of the fact (to prove a negative here would require citing the entire literature). However, it can be documented in the translations of original Ch'an texts, and that is the project of this Appendix.

Translators of Ch'an texts have not understood the conceptual framework of original Ch'an (not surprising for the early translators, as they were our culture's first encounter with a radically different way of thinking). And so, they have not recognized key philosophical concepts or understood how to translate them—whether in the terminology itself, or in how those concepts infuse the language more generally. These clearly defined and empirical concepts were either untranslated or translated with a mélange of vague and often meaninglessly abstract terms that often introduce metaphysical assumptions found in Indian Buddhism or Western philosophy. But metaphysical dimensions of any kind are entirely foreign to empirically based Ch'an understanding. Remarkably, translators also routinely use different terms to translate the same Chinese concept, even in a single passage. And to compound this, there is a general failure to understand translation's task to respect original texts by rendering them on their own terms with precision and literary sensitivity. Instead, we often find loose paraphrase and restatement according to translators' unrecognized assumptions and misunderstandings about the nature of Ch'an.

The original texts cited in this book are a tiny sampling generally chosen to represent the full chronological sweep of the tradition, and also taken primarily from the most prominent figures, those who exist in English translations that have exerted substantial influence on American Zen's understanding of itself. Comparisons of those translations with the more philosophically accurate translations given in this book (all of which are my own) reveal how the earlier translations misrepresent Ch'an's native cosmology. These comparative translations appear below in this Appendix. They are referenced with endnote numbers in the text. When multiple translations are listed, they appear in chronological order, to give a sense of how translators either repeated or differed from earlier strategies. The numbers following translators' names give page numbers for the citations in the source texts. If more than one text is referenced for a single translator, the page number is preceded by the number of the text as given in the list of source texts, which appears after the Appendix.

1. Influential translations of the Taoist classics, root-source of Ch'an's conceptual framework, also misrepresent Taoism's foundational concepts. In translating 無, they inevitably

138

impose a vague metaphysical realm wholly foreign to Taoism and Ch'an, using terms like *not being* and *nothing*.

2. Suzuki (3: 196): "see into nothingness." He then goes on to explain this nothingness as a state in which "not a thing is," suggesting a vaguely metaphysical realm completely foreign to Ch'an.

3. This cosmological/ontological sense of 意 appears often in Ch'an texts, but it is generally lost in translation, replaced by such terms as "mind," "consciousness," "conceptual consciousness," "thought," "meaning," "secret meaning," "cardinal meaning," "truly important."

4. Blofeld (106):

> So if I now state that there are no phenomena and no Original Mind, you will begin to understand something of the intuitive Dharma silently conveyed to Mind with Mind.

Here is a strange metaphysics having nothing to do with Ch'an or the original text. It is the translation, and not the original, making the assertion that reality both empirical and mental somehow doesn't exist. The distortion is only compounded in the claim that this non-existence is the essential insight of Ch'an, the "Dharma silently conveyed." This is the kind of incomprehensibility that is so often presented as a Zen essence the intuiting of which represents enlightenment.

5. 無 ("Absence") is never discussed in its Taoist sense as a cosmological/ontological concept in English-language books by modern Zen teachers. And in modern translations of Ch'an texts, 無 is never translated in that native Taoist sense. It is often left untranslated. Sometimes it is simply left

in its Japanese pronunciation *mu* (see p. 53 f.), which erases the concept entirely (and also represents an act of cultural appropriation, presenting Chinese Ch'an as Japanese). And sometimes it is translated as "no/not." "No/not" is a common meaning for 無, and so is sometimes correct. But this translation is very often used when the term is clearly meant in its philosophical sense, and when the word is meant to have both meanings simultaneously, which is very often the case in an array of crucial philosophical terms, as we will see. When recognized as a philosophical concept, it is translated with terms like "non-being," "non-existence," "void," all of which introduce a metaphysical realm familiar to Indian Buddhism, but that has nothing to do with Ch'an's radical empiricism.

6. The Chinese title of the *Mind Sutra* is 心經, which is generally mistranslated into English as the *Heart Sutra*. 心 means "heart" and "mind" as a single entity (see p. 39), and "heart" alone has apparently been chosen for emotional appeal. But in Ch'an, 心 should almost always be translated "mind" because the emphasis is on consciousness empty of all contents, rather than emotions. And indeed, the *Mind Sutra* focuses with great concision on Absence/emptiness as the essential nature of mind that must be understood for awakening.

The poem begins with a long incantation on *emptiness* (空), including lines like:

This beautiful world of things,
this world is no different than emptiness,
and emptiness no different than this world,
this world exactly emptiness,
emptiness exactly this world.
Our perceptions and thoughts, actions and distinctions:
they too are all like this.

In translations, this emptiness is widely assumed to have the kind of metaphysical implications it would have in Indian Buddhism, suggesting everything is illusory, etc. But in its native Taoist framework, *emptiness* is synonymous with *Absence*, which makes the sutra's proposition quite precise and empirical.

In addition to emptiness, the other repeated term in this passage is 色 (*se*). In the numerous existing translations, 色 is always translated as "form," hence translations like this by Roshi Robert Aitken, which is virtually the same as other translations by people like D. T. Suzuki or Red Pine: "form is no other than emptiness, emptiness no other than form; / form is exactly emptiness, emptiness exactly form" (2:110).

Such translations invest the *Mind Sutra* with an impossibly vague metaphysics that typifies Indian Buddhism, and that had little appeal to the empirical-minded Chinese, for *form* can only be read as an abstract metaphysical concept that somehow shapes or informs the physical realm. But in fact, 色 means "color" or "beauty/appearance," as in a beautiful and even seductive woman. Hence, the sense is very physical and tangible and sensual: "this beautiful world of things," or perhaps "the beautiful things of this world."

The emptiness sequence is followed by the even more in cantatory sequence referenced in this note, where 無 replaces 空 ("emptiness") as the rhythmic drumbeat. The Chinese 無 also means "no/not," that simple grammatical function word. As we see again and again, that double meaning is often exploited in philosophical concepts, and here it allows 無 to be read throughout either in its simple meaning of "not" or in its cosmological/ontological meaning, "Absence." Reading 無 as "not," the passage reads as a series of negations, which is how translators have always rendered it and which gives the following in Aitken's translation:

141

Therefore, in emptiness there is no form, no sensation,
  thought, impulse, consciousness;
no eye, ear, nose, tongue, body, mind;
no color, sound, smell, taste, touch, object of thought;
no realm of sight to no realm of thought;
no ignorance and also no ending of ignorance
to no old age and death and also no ending of old age
  and death (2:110)

But read only this way, it again describes some kind of imagined metaphysical realm that is perhaps known through awakening and is more true than the physical world. The empirically minded Chinese would have had no patience for such claims.

Hence, we are encouraged to read 無 as the this-worldly Taoist concept of Absence, the physical world seen as a single generative tissue. This reading is also suggested because between the poem's "emptiness" section and "Absence" section, there is a sentence full of negations in which the more common negation word 不 is used. So the sudden switch to 無 rather than continuing with 不 suggests that we read 無 as "Absence." And further: the more this passage is read as poetic incantation—and the *Mind Sutra* is routinely chanted by Ch'an practitioners—the more 無 resonates as "Absence." This empiricist and incantatory reading gives lines like my translation in the main text that is referenced by this note:

And so, in emptiness this beautiful world of things is
  Absence,
perceptions Absence, thoughts, actions, distinctions,
Absence eyes and ears, nose and tongue, self and meaning and *ch'i*-mind itself,
Absence this beautiful dharma-world,
its color and sound, smell and taste and touch,
Absence the world of sight

and even the world of *ch'i*-mind, its meanings and
  distinctions,
Absence Absence-wisdom
and Absence Absence-wisdom extinguished,
Absence old-age unto death
and Absence old-age unto death extinguished.

The poetic effectiveness of the passage, as it would have been
read by the ancient Chinese masters, is how the two readings
exist simultaneously. And in fact, the two are complementary,
for when the world is seen as Absence, there are indeed no
individuated things as when 無 is read as "not," making the
sequence a list of negations.

7. Blofeld (34):

Mind in itself is not mind, yet neither is it no-mind. To say
that Mind is no-mind implies something existent.

Here we see Ch'an's conceptual approach again replaced by a
mélange of Indian Buddhism and Western philosophy, for the
translation posits mind as something "non-existent," as somehow transcendental. But that seems barely significant compared to the complete erasure of the foundational concepts
Absence and Presence. (The second meaning of 無 as "no/
not" operates here, but only secondarily.)

Similarly, to take another random but representative sample,
one among countless, here is another passage from Blofeld's
translation (106): "Once more, ALL phenomena are basically
without existence, though you cannot now say that they are
NON-EXISTENT. Karma having arisen does not thereby
exist; karma destroyed does not thereby cease to exist."

Translated accurately within its native philosophical framework and respecting the essential Ch'an spirit of dismantling

143

all concepts, the passage reads like this: "The dharma of all things is not fundamentally Presence, and it's also not Absence. What has arisen from the origin-tissue is not Presence, and what has vanished back into the origin-tissue is not Absence."

This is challenging philosophically, but the Blofeld version can only be described as wisdom-nonsense. In it, Ch'an's foundational ideas are absent and/or misshapen, and a kind of metaphysics is introduced into this strictly empirical ontology/cosmology. The translation sees Ch'an through the lens of Indian Buddhism (when Ch'an in fact dismantles the ideas of that tradition), not just with the metaphysics in which nothing exists but also with the complete mistranslation of 緣 as the trendy "karma" when it means "source" or, more fully: "origin-tissue."

8. Translations of this dramatically direct declaration (Blythe, Shibayama, Sekida, Aitken, Yamada) are another striking example of Ch'an's native concepts lost in translation, for they all leave 無 ("Absence") untranslated, choosing instead to render it as the Japanese pronunciation of the word: *mu*. (Again, to say nothing of the cultural appropriation involved.) Thomas Cleary translates it simply as "no."

9. There are many translations of this widely influential poem. The early translators R. H. Blythe and Arthur Waley realized there are philosophical dimensions in this passage, but they introduced a metaphysical realm of "non-being," and otherwise didn't understand or render what the Chinese was saying:

Blythe (1: ch. 3): So too with Being and non-Being.

Waley (298): Being is an aspect of Non-being; Non-being is an aspect of Being.

Suzuki (2: 81–2) changes the terminology, but not the imposed metaphysical realm:

144

What is is the same with what is not,
What is not is the same with what is.

Later translators, including Watson and a host of Zen teachers, generally followed one of these two strategies. One noteworthy variation, with its own version of metaphysical imposition, is Andy Ferguson's recent translation (502):

Existence is but emptiness,
Emptiness, existence.

10. Blofeld (43) here imposes the same metaphysics as Ferguson (above):

If only you will avoid concepts of existence and non-existence in regard to absolutely everything, you will then perceive the DHARMA.

As Blofeld's translation is an influential antecedent, it is perhaps part of the reason for the assumptions that led to later mistranslations like Ferguson's.

11. This poem from No-Gate's Forward offers another example of how the Taoist ontology/cosmology of Absence and Presence is erased in translation, for translators all take 無 to mean simply "no," as in Roshi Robert Aitken's version (1: 4):

The Great Way has no gate;
there are a thousand different paths;
once you pass through the barrier,
you walk the universe alone.

The other translations are all very close to this. And none translate Absence's complement, "Presence," where it appears in the second line. But translated in its native philosophical framework, the poem looks like this:

The great Way is a single Absence-gate
here on a thousand roads of Presence.

Once through this gateway, you wander
all heaven and earth in a single stride.

12. In the two primary translations, the cosmological/ontological
concept is lost when 無 is translated as "void" (Sasaki 165)
and "no fixed form" (Watson 3: 25–6):

If the mind is void, wherever you are, you are emancipated.

And because this single mind has no fixed form, it is everywhere in a state of emancipation.

13. Translations of *tzu-jan*, a precisely defined concept in Taoist/
Ch'an thought, vary widely and in considerable confusion, including: "what we are," "So-in-itself," "nature," "naturalness,"
"genuine character," "own nature," "Supreme Enlightenment,"
"fruition," "spontaneous," "familiar."

14. Yampolsky and Red Pine (this passage is not included in the
text used by Cleary and McRae) lose the Taoist cosmological/
ontological dimensions of the awakening that Prajna-Able is
describing when they translate 意 (*"ch'i*-thought/mind":
pp. 39–40) simply as "cardinal meaning" and "truly important" (italicized):

Yampolsky (132): "If you do not know the original mind,
studying the Dharma is to no avail. If you know the mind and
see its true nature, you then awaken to the *cardinal meaning*."

Red Pine (2: 8): "Unless you know your own mind, studying
the Dharma is useless. But once you know your mind and see
your nature, you understand what is *truly important*."

15. The major translators of Ch'an texts use a startling range of terms to translate 理 (inner-pattern), all vague abstractions giving no hint of the actual philosophical concept: "reason," "principle," "truth," "true principle," "inner truth." In a footnote explaining 理, which he has translated as "Reason," Suzuki (2: 73) gives these alternate meanings for the concept: "Higher Intuition," "Conduct," "Practical Living."

16. Translators muddle these key passages with inaccuracy and vague abstraction:
    Suzuki (1: 181–2): "in silent communion with the principle ["Reason" in Suzuki's earlier translation (2: 72)] itself . . . free from conceptual discrimination . . . understand the truth . . . the wise."
    Thomas Cleary (1: 5–6): "tacitly merging with the Way . . . [untranslated] . . . the true principle is contrary to the mundane . . . heroes of the Way."
    J. C. Cleary (34–5): "This is tacit accord with the real inner truth . . . without discrimination . . . using inner truth . . . the wise awaken to the real."
    Red Pine (2: 3–4) "complete and unspoken agreement with reason . . . [untranslated] . . . choose reason over custom . . . the wise wake up."
    Foster (4): "Complete, ineffable accord with the Principle . . . without discrimination . . . going with the Principle . . . the wise awaken to the truth."
    Foster offers a suggestive but still vague and inaccurate footnote: "Principle (li) is a central concept in classical Chinese thought, where it refers to the cosmic order."

17. Dragon-Lake's final question ("You just saw the inner-pattern of Way. Tell me, what is it?") is reduced by translators to the

147

following variations, several later translations apparently copying the distinctive error of the first:

Blythe (199): "What have you realized?"

Shibayama (201): "What realization do you have?"

Sekida (93): "What sort of realization did you have?"

Aitken (1: 177): "What truth did you discern?"

Thomas Cleary (3: 132): "What principle have you seen?"

Yamada (136): "What have you realized?"

18. For comparison:

Suzuki (1: 82): "the reason in its essence is pure which we call the Dharma"

Thomas Cleary (1: 7): "the truth of the purity of nature." [*Truth* here translates 法 (*dharma*), 理 (*inner-pattern*) is untranslated.]

J. C. Cleary (36): "The Dharma, the Teaching of Reality, is based on the inner truth of the inherent purity [of all things' true identity]."

[bracketed clarification is Cleary's]

Red Pine (7): "The Dharma is the truth that all natures are pure."

Foster (5): "The principle of essential purity is the Dharma."

Broughton (11): "The practice of according with Dharma, the principle of intrinsic purity is viewed as Dharma."

19. As we have seen with so many root concepts, 玄 ("dark-enigma") is often left untranslated, or is translated with a mélange of misleading and falsely mystifying terms in English (the word-choice, again, often changing within a single text), such as:

Suzuki: "deep mystery"

Waley: "mystery"

Blythe: "deep mystery"

Shibayama: untranslated, "various profound philosophies," "underbrush"

Sasaki: "mysterious principle," "deep and mysterious"

Sekida: untranslated, "all the secrets of the world," "profundity"

Aitken: untranslated, "abstruse doctrines," "darkness of abandoned grasses" [following Shibayama]

Thomas Cleary: "mystic discernment," "the hidden"

Watson: "Dark Meaning," "secret meaning," "profound and abstruse," "dark in entity"

Yamada: untranslated, "abstruse doctrine," "grasses" [following Shibayama and Aitken]

20. In the following translations that thoroughly misrepresented the original, the root concepts are italicized, appearing in this order: *dharma* (法), *existence-tissue* (如), *dark-enigma* (玄), *existence-tissue* (如), *emptiness* (虛), *dharma* (法), *tzu-jan* (自然).

Suzuki (2: 80):

> If the mind retains its oneness,
> The ten thousand *things* are of one *Suchness*.
> When the *deep mystery* of one *Suchness* is fathomed,
> All of a sudden we forget the *external entanglements*:
> When the ten thousand *things* are viewed in their
> oneness,
> We return to the origin and remain *what we are*.

Waley (297):

> If the mind makes no distinctions all *Dharmas*
> become *one*.
> Let *the One* with its *mystery* blot out all memory of
> *complications*.

149

Let the thought of the *Dharmas* as All-One bring you
to the *So-in-itself.*

Blythe (1: ch. 3):

If the mind makes no discriminations,
All *things* are *as they really are.*

In the *deep mystery* of this "things *as they are,"*
We are released from our relations to *them.*
When all *things* are seen "with equal mind,"
They return to their *nature.*

Watson (2: 150):

When the mind refrains from differentiation,
the ten thousand *phenomena* are a single *Suchness,*
a single *Suchness dark in entity,*
lumpish, forgetful of *entanglements.*

View the ten thousand *phenomena* as equal
and all will revert to *naturalness.*

Foster (14):

If you don't conjure up differences,
    all *things* are of *one kind.*
In the *essential mystery* of *identity,*
    eternal and ephemeral are forgotten.
Seeing the *things* of the world evenly
    restores their *genuine character.*

Ferguson (501):

If the mind does not go astray
The myriad *dharmas* are but *One,*
And the *One* encompasses the *Mystery.*

In stillness, *conditioned existence* is forgotten,
And the myriad *things* are seen equally,
Naturally returning to each one's *own nature.*

21. For comparison:

Sasaki (183): ". . . grasp and use, but never name—this is called the 'mysterious principle.'"

Watson (3: 30): ". . . get hold of this thing and use it, but don't fix a label to it. This is what I call the Dark Meaning."

22. For comparison:

Sasaki (206): "in control of every circumstance . . . this very man of the Way, dependent upon nothing . . . mysterious principle of all the buddhas."

Watson (3: 40): "to master the environment . . . a man of the Way who has learned to lean on nothing . . . the secret meaning of the buddhas."

23. For comparison:

Sasaki (247): "the buddhadharma is deep and mysterious"

Watson (3. 56): "The Dharma of the buddhas is profound and abstruse"

24. For comparison:

Blythe (303): "Getting rid of your illusions and penetrating into the truth . . ."

Shibayama (316): "To inquire after the Truth, groping your way through the underbrush, is for the purpose of seeing into your nature."

[Shibayama repeats his mistaken translation of 玄 (*dark-enigma*) as "underbrush," and Aitken and Yamada again follow.]

151

Sekida (131): "You leave no stone unturned to explore profundity, simply to see into your true nature."

Aitken (1: 278): "You make your way through the darkness of abandoned grasses in a single-minded search for your self-nature."

Thomas Cleary (3: 204): "Brushing aside confusion to search out the hidden is only for the purpose of seeing essence."

Yamada (220): "The purpose of making one's way through grasses and asking a master about the subtle truth is only to realize one's self-nature."

25. It's important to note that here, as normal in classical Chinese, there is no *you/your* in the original. Personal pronouns like this, necessary in English and rare in classical Chinese, create an illusory self separate from everything else, a proposition that exactly contradicts the liberation described in this passage.

26. *Wu-wei* is generally translated with some variation on the idea of "non-action." Although seemingly literal, that translation completely misrepresents the concept, turning it into a kind of monkish passivity. In fact, the import is quite the opposite: action that is selfless, spontaneous, and even wild. When there is some awareness of the philosophical concept, the translations fail to render the concept at all: "the uncreated" (Suzuki), "nameless" (Cleary), "the sublime" (Red Pine). In addition, translators often use starkly different terms to translate the same *wu-wei*, even when it occurs within the same passage. Specific examples can be found in the next two notes.

27. Words translating *wu-wei* are italicized:
Suzuki (1: 180): "serene and *not-acting*"
Thomas Cleary (1: 5): "silently *not-doing*"

152

J. C. Cleary (34): "still and *nameless*"

Red Pine (3: 3): "Without moving, *without effort*"

Foster (4): "still, *effortless*"

28. In this passage, which in the original Bodhidharma text comes only a few paragraphs below the passage noted above, the translators all use entirely different terms (again italicized) to translate the same *wu-wei*:

Suzuki (1: 182): "Their minds abide serenely in the *uncreated*."

Thomas Cleary (1: 12): "their minds at ease, *without striving*"

J. C. Cleary (35): "Pacifying mind without *contrived activity*."

Red Pine (3: 5): "They fix their minds on the *sublime*."

Foster (4): "Peaceful at heart, with *nothing to do*."

29. For comparison:

Suzuki (1: 199): "The wise are non-active."

Waley (297): "Those who know most, do least."

Blythe (1: 83): "The wise man does nothing."

Watson (2: 150): "Wise men take no special action."

Ferguson (501): "The wise do not move."

30. The standard translations of the final sentence contradict what's come before and introduce *Dhyana* Buddhism's focus on cultivating a mental state of nirvana-tranquility, apparently because the translators assume that Ch'an is essentially a form of Indian *dhyana* Buddhism. Their misreading of the original mistakenly describes thoughts as a violation of *dhyana* purity and stillness, thereby proposing exactly what Prajna-Able is arguing against here. For him, mind is "original source-tissue purity" even when preoccupied with "illusory thoughts" that "hide" the world from us.

153

Yampolsky (139): "If someone speaks of "viewing purity," [then I would say] that man's nature is of itself pure, and because of false thoughts True Reality is obscured."

[bracketed clarification is Yampolsky's]

Thomas Cleary (2: 35): "If you speak of fixating on purity, people's essential nature is originally pure; it is by false thoughts that they cover reality as such..."

McRae (59): "If one is to concentrate on purity, then [realize that because] our natures are fundamentally pure, it is through false thoughts that suchness is covered up."

[bracketed clarification is McRae's]

Red Pine (2: 14–5): "If someone says to contemplate purity, your nature is already pure. It's because of deluded thoughts that reality is obscured."

31. For comparison:

Yampolsky (139): "'Thought' means thinking of the original nature of True Reality. True Reality is the substance of thoughts; thoughts are the function of True Reality. If you give rise to thoughts from your self-nature, then, although you see, hear, perceive, and know, you are not stained by the manifold environments, and are always free."

Thomas Cleary (2: 33): "'Thought' means thought of the original nature of reality as such. Reality as such is the substance of thought, thought is the function of reality as such. The intrinsic nature of reality as such produces thought. [Cleary translated from a different text that has additional material here] ... the essential nature of reality as such produces thought. Though the six senses have perception and cognition, the real essential nature is not affected by myriad objects; it is always independent."

McRae (59): "Thought is to think of the fundamental nature of suchness. Suchness is the essence of thought, thought

154

is the function of suchness. Thought is activated in the self-nature of suchness . . . [McRae translated from a different text that has additional material here] . . . thoughts are activated from the self-nature of suchness. Although the six sensory faculties possess perceptual cognition, they do not defile the myriad realms. And yet the true nature is always autonomous."

Red Pine (2:13): "And 'thought' is thought about the original nature of reality. Reality is the body of thought, and thought is the function of reality. When your nature gives rise to thought, even though you sense something, remain free and unaffected by the world of objects."

32. For comparison:

Watson (1: 94): "Let your mind wander in simplicity, blend your spirit with the vastness, follow along with things the way they are, and make no room for personal views . . ."

Graham (90): "Let your heart roam in the flavourless, blend your energies with the featureless, in the spontaneity of your accord with other things leave no room for selfishness . . ."

33. The final clause ("Absence's own doing/action [wu-wei] wandering boundless and free through the selfless unfolding of things") becomes in the standard translations:

Watson (1: 87): ". . . they wander free and easy in the service of inaction."

Graham (90): ". . . go rambling through the lore in which there's nothing to *do*"

34. For comparison:

Sasaki (199): "return to impermanence"

Watson (3: 36): "headed for the impermanence that awaits us all"

35. Blofeld (80):

If you could prevent all conceptual movements of thought and still your thinking-processes, naturally there would be no error left in you. Therefore it is said: "When thoughts arise, then do all things arise. When thoughts vanish, then do all things vanish."

Here the Taoist/Ch'an conceptual framework is lost in the first sentence when *tzu-jan* is translated simply and inaccurately as "naturally," and "unborn" becomes "prevent." This and the absence of "dharma" makes the quoted saying sound like it is some kind of idealism in which the physical world is a creation of the human mind. This metaphysics pervades the Blofeld translation—as in "pure Mind, the source of everything" (p. 36), which seems to be proposing a universal God-consciousness or again some kind of idealism in which physical reality is a creation of the human mind. But the text actually says something like "this pure-clarity source-tissue mind of origins," referring to empty-mind as generative Absence. Blofeld's imposed metaphysics is quite the opposite of Ch'an principles. As is the forced struggle to "prevent" thought, and also the judgmental and moralistic "no error"—both exactly what Yellow-Bitterroot Mountain is arguing against.

36. Blofeld (130) here misses both of the big concepts, "non-birth" and "*tzu-jan* occurrence." And once more, falsely assuming "no-birth" somehow refers to "conceptual thought and intellectual processes" not mentioned in the original (hence his brackets), he imposes *dhyana* quietism on Ch'an (again, the opposite of what Yellow-Bitterroot Mountain proposes):

When [conceptual thought and intellectual processes] no longer trouble you, you will unfailingly reach Supreme Enlightenment.

37. Compare Blofeld (127):

Only when your minds cease dwelling upon anything what-
soever will you come to an understanding of the true way
of Zen.

38. Compare Poceski (312):

When (a person) comes to apprehend (the true nature of)
the mind and the external objects, then there is no more
arising of deluded thinking. When deluded thinking is not
created anymore, that is precisely the acceptance (of reality based on cognition) of the uncreated nature of things.
It originally exists, and it exists in the present moment, not
being something that is dependent on spiritual cultivation
or sitting meditation. When there is no more (attachment
to) practice and sitting, that is precisely the untainted
meditation of the Tathagata (Buddha).

39. Other translations leave 無 (Absence) untranslated, rendering it simply as the Japanese pronunciation: *mu*. (This is
true for all instances of 無 in *No-Gate Gateway*, though it is
clearly the central concept of the book.) And so, they lose the
cosmological/ontological dimensions of what is involved in
this awakening.

The crucial concept of *tzu-jan* in this phrase ("nurture the
simplicity of occurrence appearing of itself [*tzu-jan*]") is left
out in all other translations of *No-Gate Gateway*, most done
by modern Zen roshis, two of whom repeat Blythe's mistaken
"fruition." Terms used to translate *tzu-jan* are italicized.

Blythe (32): "After a certain period of time, this striving will
come to *fruition naturally* . . ."

Shibayama (19): "when your efforts come to *fruition*"

Sekida (28): "and when the time comes" [*tzu-jan* un-
translated]

157

Aitken (1: 9): [entire phrase untranslated]

Thomas Cleary (3: 2): "Washing away your previous misconceptions and misperceptions, eventually it becomes thoroughly *familiar*"

Yamada (12): "After a certain period of such efforts, Mu will come to *fruition*"

TEXTS REFERENCED
IN APPENDIX

Aitken, Robert: 1. *The Gateless Barrier* (1990)
                      2. *Taking the Path of Zen* (1982)
Blofeld, John: *The Zen Teaching of Huang Po* (1958)
Blythe, R. H.:   1. *Zen and Zen Classics, Vol. 1* (1960)
                      2. *Zen and Zen Classics, Vol. 4:*
                         Mumonkan (1966)
Broughton, Jeffrey: *The Bodhidharma Anthology* (1999)
Cleary, J. C.:   *Zen Dawn* (1986)
Cleary, Thomas: 1. *Sayings and Doings of Pai-chang*
                         (1978)
                      2. *The Sutra of Hui Neng* (1998)
                      3. *Unlocking the Zen Koan: A New*
                         Translation of the Zen Classic
                         Wumenkuan (1993)
Ferguson, Andy: *Zen's Chinese Heritage* (2011)
Foster, Nelson: *The Roaring Stream* (1996)
Graham, A. C.:   *Chuang Tzu: The Inner Chapters* (1981)
McRae, John: *The Platform Sutra of the Sixth*
                      Patriarch (2000)
Poceski, Mario: *The Records of Mazu and the Making of*
                      Classical Chan Literature (2015)

Red Pine: 1. *The Heart Sutra* (2004)
2. *The Platform Sutra* (2006)
3. *The Zen Teaching of Bodhidharma* (1987)

Sasaki, Ruth: *The Record of Lin-Chi* (1975) (Page numbers refer to expanded 2009 edition.)

Sekida, Katsuki: *Two Zen Classics* (1977)

Shibayama, Zenkai: *The Gateless Barrier* (1974)

Suzuki, D. T.:   1. *Essays in Zen Buddhism, First Series* (1949)
2. *Manual of Zen Buddhism* (1935/1960)
3. *Zen Buddhism: Selected Writings of D. T. Suzuki* (1956)

Tanahashi, Kazuaki: *The Heart Sutra* (2014)

Waley, Arthur: "On Trust in the Heart" in *Buddhist Texts Through the Ages*, Edward Conze, ed. (1954)

Watson, Burton: 1. *The Complete Works of Chuang Tzu* (1968)
2. "On Trust in the Mind" in *Entering the Stream: An Introduction to the Buddha and His Teachings*, Samuel Bercholz and Sherab Chödzin Kohn, eds. (1993)
3. *The Zen Teachings of Master Lin-chi* (1993)

Yamada, Koun: *The Gateless Gate* (2004)

Yampolsky, Philip: *The Platform Sutra of the Sixth Patriarch* (1967)

Phil Dera

DAVID HINTON has published numerous books of poetry and essays and many translations of ancient Chinese poetry and philosophy. These translations have earned wide acclaim for creating compelling contemporary texts that convey the literary texture and philosophical density of the originals. This work earned Hinton a Guggenheim Fellowship, numerous fellowships from NEA and NEH, and both of the major awards given for poetry translation in the United States: the Landon Translation Award (Academy of American Poets) and the PEN American Translation Award. The first translator in over a century to translate the five seminal masterworks of Chinese philosophy—*I Ching, Tao Te Ching, Chuang Tzu, Analects,* and *Mencius*—Hinton was recently given a lifetime achievement award by the American Academy of Arts and Letters.